A Logical Approach To Data Management:

3 Questions

Other Books by The Author

Fundamentals of Life
Know Yourself, Be Yourself
Copyright © 2020 Sorenson Studios
Paperback ISBN: 978-0-9856781-2-8
Hardcover ISBN: 978-0-9856781-3-5
eBook ISBN: 978-0-9856781-5-9

Coffee Table Philosophy
A Book of Photos and Thoughts
First edition Copyright © 2011 Sorenson Studios
Second edition Copyright © 2020 Sorenson Studios
ISBN: 978-0-9856781-1-1

A Logical Approach To Data Management

3 Questions

Rick Sorenson

A Logical Approach To Data Management

Published by Sorenson Studios

Paperback ISBN: 978-0-9856781-6-6
Hardcover ISBN: 978-0-9856781-8-0
eBook ISBN: 978-0-9856781-9-7

Library of Congress Control Number: 2021918034

Acknowlegements

I want to thank all of my colleagues that contributed to my life and my learnings, and made this book possible. This includes people very knowledgeable in the field of data. It equally includes friends that know little of the complexity of data as well as people that may have provided my efforts with a great deal of challenge. I do not have the space to list all names but I offer you an honest thank you. You know who you are.

Thank you!

Table of Contents

PREFACE

A Little About the Author

Why This Book Now?

I have been involved with computer systems and data from some very early days. In 1970, I was writing punch tape programs in high school to run via a phone line on a mainframe in Minneapolis. I have spent the last 25 years directly involved with data and its management in various roles. These roles included Director of Data Integration, Data Governance Lead, and Data Consultant regarding strategies toward compliance to privacy laws. I have also testified in court regarding data and co-authored patent applications for data technologies and process innovations.

Throughout my career a couple of things happened. In addition to the growing passion and respect for data itself, it became obvious to me that the major challenges with managing data were not technical. Many of them were not complex. They were consistently a relatively small set of basics that were not being applied to data. Many seemed very "simple" to remedy and yet they were not. Clearly the things that seemed obvious to me were either not obvious to others or there was something else driving the behavior that was seen as more important. I was driven, out of frustration and a need to understand, to look further at why this happens and what could be done about it.

My two previous books have been philosophy books, so what I am doing writing a data book? These are much more aligned than they might seem on the surface. My approach to managing data is one of logic, and philosophy is based on logic. Dissecting information to draw a conclusion is important to both. Understanding the factors involved in the "inputs" to the computation is critical.

My experience, along with the experience of colleagues in the business of data, has led me to conclusions that are not rocket science but certainly have escaped many. These concepts are simple; however, the execution can seem like an insurmountable task causing people to fail or even not try. My goal, as with all of my books, is to help others. I hope that my experience, observations, and conclusions expressed in this book will provide you with some insight into the possibilities and challenges in regard to managing data. I hope that you will see data slightly different and be able to apply these concepts, not only to your business, but also to all data from all sources. I believe that we can all do better at distinguishing between the various degrees of reliability of data and its resulting conclusions. Not all data is fact.

INTRODUCTION

Data management is a *very* broad topic and it is *much* more than a technical task. The logical approach to managing data can have an impact on more than just the task of managing data. Managing data has a purpose that serves all that touch data.

The purpose of this book is to share an overall approach for managing data from beginning to end and potentially a new way of even thinking about data. It is intentionally not a technical or a technology-specific book. The logic, patterns, and requirements discussed are technology-agnostic.

It is best to take a little time to discuss just one word in the title of this book; data. Is this really a book about data management? What is the difference between data and information? If you search the Internet, you will find a vast array of opinions and definitions of the difference. Regardless of which way I went with the title of this book and the use of the terms within, I risked missing part of the intended audience. For the true data technologists, this is likely an information management book and they may be irritated by my use of the data management term. On the other hand, for those that are not of that background (of which there are many more), using information rather than data takes on a perception that may cause a larger group to be missed. Most people will use "data" when talking about either data or information. The terms blur. Information, to many, is a conclusion that is drawn from data and I don't want to give the perception that this book is strictly about conclusions of data such as reporting or analytics. I could try to be "pure" in definition or focus on the meaning rather than the label. That is true for many words and most communication issues in the world, and that is the path that we will take. We will spend some time in the first chapter with the definition of "data" as it is being used in this book.

Data has grown so fast and the push to use the data in new ways has far outweighed the logical approach of understanding the data before using it. The push to "use" forces assumptions, and assumptions become the culture. When it is engrained in the culture, nobody sees them as assumptions, but rather they are seen as facts. They are embedded in the operations as fact. When you use the principles and methodology in this book to force a common understanding and singular definition of data, you find that there are many versions of a single fact. Logically that is impossible, so what happens? In many cases, it has been ignored because it is too difficult to understand; how could so much data have been wrong and yet there seems to be "success" in using the data? You end up with behavioral conditioning, believing that conflicting data (meaning that some of it is wrong) is okay. This is just one of the scenarios that makes data management change difficult.

The concept of data management being difficult is one of the major deterrents to the implementation of data management. It may have been tried and failed. The failure is not a failure of data management, but rather a failure of the approach.

So, why this approach? Managing data is likely to be a cultural shift due to rapid technology advancements, the explosion of data, and the inability to adapt management to these changing realities. Cultural shifts take time and consistency, and a technical approach will not be stable over an extended period of time. How many times do you suspect that the technologies touching data change during the life of the data? In order to manage data, the approach must be stable and grounded in a way that can be consistent, regardless of the people or technologies that may change around it.

Data is everything! Is that too strong? Depending on the context it might be, but let me explain. From a personal level, I am not going to tell you that data is more important than family, friends, health, or your beliefs. However, from a business perspective I believe that data is *the most important* component of business. You can't have inventory, finances, managed customers, etc. without data. You cannot accurately plan a future direction or assess the past without data. It has this level of importance and yet many companies treat data as a commodity rather than with the respect that it needs.

Some of the things in this book may seem like rudimentary concepts and silly to talk about. Logical concepts seem to have that feel of being basic and obvious, yet it is not what happens. My experience and the shared experience of others tells me that the core issues with data management lie in the most basic concepts. We will start there and expand to methods of implementation. Who would use data that does not have a meaning identified? The truth is that many would and many do. Some realize it and ignore it, while many others are not aware and have fallen into a false sense of security and stability.

It has been said that knowledge is power. Knowledge comes from information and information comes from (or is) data. Data has always been important, but its importance is growing exponentially as the world evolves. Data used to be word of mouth and then written words and has evolved into massive amounts of digital data. More and more data is being created, collected, and stored. The purpose of that data is almost limitless. The decisions being made from data in the name of having "proof" or in the name of "science" grow as well. In most cases, data is your only defense.

To put this another way, data can be used to create *anything* and the power to do that only increases as the data becomes more granular and increases in volume. Data can not only be used to create reports and projects, it can become entertainment, music, movies, your complete means of communication, a building, and even a person. Think about that and where it has gone so rapidly. The reason that you have data today may be very different tomorrow, and the use of that data may become even more critical. The impact of the accuracy or inaccuracy of data may have unforeseen consequences in the future.

The threat to identity, privacy, incorrect conclusions, and manipulation increases as the data grows and spreads. One of the most important aspects to understand is that the quality of data, in many cases, is suspect at best.

It is not just the collection of data that is suspect. How is the data stored and protected? How is it transferred? How is it used? With whom is it shared? What conclusions are drawn from the data and how are those conclusions used? There are details within each of those questions that can create havoc with the data. If you combine just those factors and all their permutations with the "spin" that people can put on data by using *parts* of data, and leaving out certain relevant information, the results are endless and everyone should be concerned about the "facts" that result.

This does not mean that *everyone* is intentionally manipulating data or has ulterior motives. At the base of all of the potential conclusions, manipulations, or misrepresentations is the existence of data and what it means. This is where we begin. Many people, organizations, and governments simply do not have a grip on their data because they don't understand how, or even why to do so. Whether it's your data, you are a consumer of the results, or you are responsible for the data and results, this book may open your eyes and help you understand what it is to *manage* your data.

This book will focus on the people and companies that collect and/or consume data, which is pretty much all businesses of any kind. Within those companies are obviously people that have data of their own. Whether you are leader in the company, a businessperson, an attorney, or a technical person, this book is for you. It is important that *all* roles involved with data understand the risks, goals, and approach.

We will present a logical and realistic approach to managing data. Managing data arguably includes any activity related to data. Some of those activities are purely technical but this is not a technology book so they will not be detailed; however, all aspects of managing data are impacted by this logical approach. Some will be impacted by new requirements, new measurements, or the recognition of the impact of their decisions on other aspects of data management and usage.

You might think, by looking at the table of contents or as you are reading, that some of the topics stray from data management. Everything in this book is about managing data. Part of the message is the common understanding of managing data and how different roles and activities have significant impacts on data management. This approach aides in the implementation of a data strategy; it also helps avoid some decisions and designs unknowingly undermining that data strategy.

We will cover some basic functions and requirements of data management, some terms (both familiar and new), a method to ease the complexity of the challenge, and a number of implementation pitfalls that may be encountered along the way. Before we can talk about how and why to address data management, we first need to understand "data". Let's start there.

Chapter 1

THE PHILOSOPHY OF DATA

When we talk about data throughout the rest of this book or as you talk about data in your daily life, it is important to understand what data is. The philosophy of data is the way that we approach data. The details of the approach will be covered in the rest of this book but we need to start with what it means to be data. When you say "data", what does it mean? Many arguments can be made about what it means in various contexts so the purpose of this chapter is to define the minimal requirements for talking about data.

Facts

Facts exist in the past and require context. The justification for this statement is based on the premise that nobody can *factually* predict the future. People can predict the future via all sorts of means and some may even call them scientific. It is possible that they are right some of the time or very close. They can make predictions, but an important distinction is that it is based on someone's beliefs, assessments, and a resulting conclusion that they believe has some level of probability. To some this may seem like semantics but when it comes to data, the difference between fact and a probability can be immense. It is absolutely fine to make decisions on probabilities as long as you know that they are probabilities and have faith in the source of the assessment. It is not fine to represent probabilities and perceptions as facts. One complication with vast amounts of data is that your source has very often passed through so many layers that even if you trust the last assessment, do you trust the one before that, or the one before that?

Let's look at a few examples of data where this concept is supported:

- You cannot hold someone accountable for a contract because you were sure they were going to sign it. The contract must have been created in the past and have a signature, a date, and in some cases witnesses. The purpose of this is to ensure that it is a fact.

- You are not allowed to pay your taxes based on how much you think you are going to make. You may be allowed to estimate taxes but you need to settle up with the facts and are expected to be able to provide proof of something that happened in the past.

- A receipt for a purchase is something that happened in the past and there are many reasons that there is a date associated with that receipt. There is financial reporting, sales tax reporting, potential returns, warranty, and customer tax deductions to name a few. The receipt is not of much value without the artifacts that make it official.

These examples are well understood and I suspect that some will challenge this concept on the basis that their type of data is "different". This is not about a different type of data; this is about the definition of data and the definition cannot be conditional. A conditional definition will never have a reliable meaning because the assessment of the condition will vary from person to person and over time, which by definition makes the data not factual but rather perception or projection. The idea of factual data is a fundamental concept.

This is not to say that projections are not valid data but they are valid perception data rather than valid raw or factual data. Companies make decisions on projections and perceptions frequently and they need to. At some point that projection should be based on raw data that is a fact.

How many steps or layers are between your projection and the raw data? We will get into much more detail on the execution of this concept throughout this book. A primary purpose of this chapter is to understand the difference between useable factual data and projections, perceptions, or probabilities.

Not all raw data is factual but if it can be a fact it should be rather than lose the factual status to incompetence, lack of effort, or failed process. Let's look at what makes raw data factual and usable.

Raw Data

Many will think of a data value as being the raw data. This data could be a number, a word, a phrase, or any set of characters that can represent a "value". That is not the raw data in this case, but it is a key component of the raw data. The data element on its own has no meaning, no function, and no purpose.

Are 1s and 0s data? Is this book data? What does 2 mean? What does n mean? They are all data but not the *complete* raw data. How would you use them? A data element needs a label. That label carries the meaning of the data element. The element is strictly a value.

That tertiary relationship between the label and the data element and between the label and the meaning looks like this:

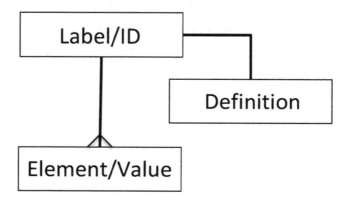

Figure 1-1

It is critical that the relationship between the label and the meaning is singular (one to one). Changes over time or conditional definitions will drift and the line between definitions will either move or more likely be forgotten. Data gets complex really fast, so it is essential to keep the raw data as simple as possible from the beginning. If not, all of the following steps of data management become exponentially complex.

In addition to the value, label, and definition, it needs some timeframe context in order for this raw data to be a fact. For that fact to be complete it also needs the context related to the source or circumstances of capture. These are the minimum requirements for raw data that is usable and worthy of respect and trust. This may seem like a lot of requirements have been added to something that carries a name of raw that implies minimal. There is a lot more information related to the raw data that can make it more useful and we will discuss that in detail, but let me give you a few examples of why this is minimal.

A receipt was used as an example for making the case for facts and it led well into the remaining attributes. The receipt will have a date and the source (name of the company purchased from). It may also enhance that source with address, store number, register number, sales clerk or other information that makes that receipt more useful. The minimum requirement for any value on that receipt remains the same. Now that we've broached the concept of a sale, consider the financial reporting and *assume* that the sales data comes from the same source as the receipt and carries as much integrity. Is that a fact or just an assumption?

Let's use inventory as the business function for another example. The value is 100. What is 100? Is it the length, the dollar value, the quantity or any one of hundreds of other things? Let's go with quantity. Now we have a label. We do not know if this is 100 items or 100 boxes or 100 pallets. We need to know that or 100 still does not mean enough. There are a number of ways to address that unit of measure, but we do need to know for the raw data to be useful. As we step through the minimal requirements for raw data, imagine that you did not know when this count was taken. How much value is the information other than at some point you could conclude that you had 100. Dates, and maybe time, are extremely important to the value and integrity of the data element (when was it captured/created?). The last requirement is the context of the capture. Is the inventory captured by reducing previous value based on sales of production use? Is it based on someone physically counting the products or some other way of counting inventory?

The complete set of relationships looks like this:

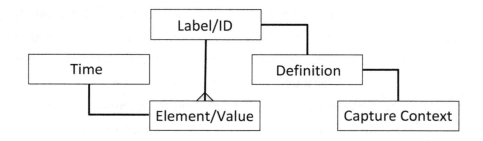

Figure 1-2

Please note that this is not intended to be a data model. It is a simple representation of the relationships. Some of the optional one-to-many relationships will be explored in other chapters. There are many ways to address the requirements but they *are required* for the raw data to have any meaning and value. Many people will believe that they know all of this based on tribal knowledge or what seems like obvious assumptions. You may be surprised.

There are also those that will say their data is different than inventory data or financial data and does not require all of this information to be useful. There are those that may also believe that this is referring to structured data in some sort of structured storage; it is not. The same requirements apply to unstructured data and to *all* data. The way it is implemented may be different. I grant that people will use data in many ways with fewer requirements but there is no exception to the minimum requirements to be factual, reliable, and defensible. Defensible is an aspect that we will talk about in depth and it will become more and more important to companies.

Caution: Not everything that you see with the same label is the same data. This leads to the concept of master data, which we will cover in the chapter on master data management.

Respect

The only way to preserve the integrity of what we have talked about so far is to treat the data with respect. Respect comes in various forms including admiration, honor, and protection. We are talking about data, right? You would preserve, defend, and protect the integrity of something or someone that you respect. You would not let someone harm or manipulate them into changing who or what they are that you respect. You would not leave it lying around or put them at risk.

Data has a life and can be very powerful and yet it cannot protect itself. It takes the stewards and custodians of the data to protect it. If it is not protected, it loses its value. This would be like you being made responsible for guarding a 200-carat diamond. You consider risks and you make sure that all aspects are protected. If someone swaps the diamond for a good replica that is glass, it may go unnoticed until someone drops it and it shatters. By the time you notice, it is too late to identify when or how it was changed.

A common statement is, "treat data as an asset". This is maybe a step in the right direction for many, but it is a step that does not reflect the full purpose of the statement. You can use an asset and expect to wear it out and replace it. Once you have lost the data, as we have defined it so far, it cannot be replaced. The growth of data and technologies increases the importance and, along with the importance, increases the risk.

Why would you or I apply a philosophy to data and apply respect to this "thing"? The answer is because it is the most important "thing" to your business. There is no business that can exist without data.

Once you get to the raw data with its relationships and time context you have facts but without the respect and preservation of integrity, the facts soon become something else. They might become opinions, suppositions, lies, or a completely different subject that went off on a tangent without telling anyone.

In order to do anything with data it is important to understand what it is, how or why it functions or exists, and to treat it with respect. This perspective is essential to creating a strategy.

Summary

All values are eligible for being data, but there are minimum requirements for data to be useful and factual. I referenced numbers and characters but this book is data. The entire content of the book is data and the entire book carries the label of the title of the book, the author of the book, and the date of copyright. It is a fact in that I wrote the contents of this book. If part of this book was removed, as in quoted, it would require the attribution of the data to move with it and remain intact as fact (and to comply with copyright laws). This is the common practice of citing that carries the title, source, author, and date information.

Data is stored in various formats and the format of storage does not change the requirements for qualifying as factual and useful data.

Treating data with respect not only recognizes its value, but helps to ensure its integrity.

Some will read this and say or think, "Yeah, yeah, yeah. Give me a break. I do all this. This is so stupid." If you think that, please think again, start asking questions, and read this book. A significant number of people in business may either believe that they do all of this or that there is someone doing it on their behalf. It is highly probable that things are not what you think. I am giving you the benefit of the doubt because some know that the requirements are not met but will pretend that they are because either it "looks good" or they believe it is "enough". Let's assume you are not of that type.

To test your alignment with these basics, try gathering a group of people in your company from a few different areas that are all knowledgeable about a particular set of data. Ask them details (real details that we will discuss later) about what the data means, how it is collected, and its source. I am certain that you will be surprised about how much difference or disagreement there will be on a set of data when you ask for the detailed meaning for each part of the data.

In order to talk about data through the rest of this book and within your scope of data, a common understanding of data and how it is addressed is needed. Addressing the data *in detail* comes with a strategy, a management process, and principles; that is where we will go in this book. This common understanding is the first essential component of getting a grip on your data. Data has to be more than just a bunch of 1s and 0s to have any value and be worthy of a stature that demands respect.

Many may think that the effort involved in this chapter's description of raw data is way too complex and may say, "We need to move faster than that." The perception that defining and managing data is a hindrance and slows the use of data is a cultural perception in most companies and is something that needs to be addressed as part of the data strategy.

Here are the highlights of this chapter:
- Data should be *factual* if possible
- Factual and usable data has a set of minimum requirements regardless of the type of data or technologies used
- Non-factual data should *not* be treated or stated as fact
- Treat data with respect

Chapter 2

DATA STRATEGY

We will take the approach of a logical process with priorities focusing on the integrity of data, accuracy, effectiveness, reduction of risk, increased efficiency, and business value in mind. These are all things that sound logical and desirable, correct? Why are so many not doing it? In part, people don't know how and the problem seems so massive that they look at the immediate need and the squeaky wheel. In addition, businesses and people are not always logical; there are bureaucratic processes, egos, emotions, and engrained behaviors that resist the change that the increase in volume, advancement of technologies, and importance of data demands.

A data strategy is the beginning of the operational implementation of a way toward logically managing data and reaping the benefits. There are many facets and steps to building and maintaining a data strategy.

Some may treat a data strategy as they would a mission statement. That is not what this refers to. I see a mission statement as being a purpose or goal, but a strategy is a comprehensive plan of execution. It is actionable, not just aspirational. It is measurable, not just directional. The word "comprehensive" is a goal in itself, so a company's first strategy might not be comprehensive purely due to logistics and resources. It does however need to be comprehensive in the breadth of impact to begin with but may not be comprehensive in detail. It must also be realistic because stating a strategy that cannot possibly be achieved only does lip service to the data and only exacerbates the culture that does not treat data with respect.

Why Do I Need a Strategy?

A documented strategy is the *only* way to succeed with data. Your strategy could be to *hope* to be *lucky* and walk away, but I am not sure I would bet on the success of that strategy. A good strategy should put you in the best position for the unseen.

Without a company-wide strategy, data will be treated as all parties see fit. I use the term "company-wide" rather than "Enterprise" because of the connotation that enterprise may have in some companies. In many companies, the word enterprise is associated with IT, such as Enterprise Architecture, Enterprise Data Storage, etc. A data strategy that is limited to IT or any other segment of the business will fail. It is that simple. *Everyone* is involved in the stewardship, collection, definition, and usage of the data. Without a comprehensive scope, each person, department, or facility will operate as they see fit and the company, along with the data, will suffer.

Data encompasses all aspects of your finances, inventory, HR processes, customers, products or services, and vendors and it is your primary defense against litigation. I could go on, but I think you get the picture. Data is your company's past, present, and future. How can you not have a strategy around it?

I can assure you that many people in your company have ideas about how the data should be used and they will each do their own thing unless there is a strategy. Some see a strategy as being limiting. Knee jerk reactions to privacy and security concerns will definitely have that feel without a strategy. A comprehensive strategy can and should be very enabling, but there may be some limitations that people are not accustomed to if there has been little oversight. The risk of saying "enabling" is that some see that as being "without any rules". We will get to that topic in much more detail, but for now the "no rules" concept is not a strategy. In fact, legally, it can no longer be a strategy.

So, why a strategy? I just mentioned the legal aspect and that is one reason. Compliance with legal requirements is a necessity if you intend to adhere to the laws of the government at all levels. Sometimes compliance begins with the fact that you have thought about managing data and have documented it. Legal compliance, however, should not be the only reason, nor should it be the primary driver. Having any *one* driver of a strategy and maintenance of data will have you chasing the next requirement rather than being prepared.

There are many reasons to have a data strategy and the importance of them may vary with companies. Here are a few:

- Maximize the value of your data
- Legal and regulatory compliance
- Reduce risk
- Reduce cost

These are all "mom and apple pie things" as I have been told. The strategy is how you will do those things. An email out to all employees telling them to do something or not do something is not a strategy. It will likely have little impact because there is no accountability, ownership, or measurability. These are all components of a data strategy.

Expectations

Expect that a data strategy is not a "one and done" effort. It must evolve, become more specific, and address new aspects of data as the culture and major technology functions change. Technology function does not mean a specific tool or a function of that tool but rather a major evolution of capabilities. The intention of a logical approach is to be technology-agnostic, but there are capability advancements that can change the landscape. Examples of those include the invention of the personal computer and mobile technologies.

Expect significant resistance. Any change will meet with resistance. Implementing a comprehensive data strategy where there was not one is likely to be more than simple change; it may be a cultural shift. It may be a cultural shift at the company level and it may be "muscle memory" for individuals that have been doing their job one way for a very long time. Either way, this can bring many negative responses. The expectations of these responses need to be considered in the strategy, its implementation, and communication.

Expect to not only find resistance but to be continually asked for justification. You will need resiliency and patience.

High-Level Approach

I have mentioned two major aspects of the approach so far:

1. The strategy must apply to the entire company. You can start with a slice off the top in the context of detail, but the strategy must be universal. To clarify, this slice would be off the top that covers the entire company with no vertical silos. Even when there are specific strategies that may be executed or owned by a specific role, it is specific to the role and not specific to a person, department, or organization. Changes to people, departments, organizations, and brands of technologies can have no impact on the strategy. Data is

too pervasive and intertwined throughout a company to allow a domino impact of changes.

2. The concept of not using a single driver for a strategy. A single driver is a bad idea and here's why. Each time a new driver comes along, the approach and focus shifts to meeting the needs of that driver. You find yourself chasing solutions rather than building capabilities that are resilient to demands and opportunities. If you understand and manage your data landscape, you can be prepared for almost anything. We will talk about three "simple" questions whose answers are needed for almost any use of data. The single driver will answer the questions specifically as needed for that driver and will likely not work for the next demand. The focus should be on the management of the data rather than a single driver or outcome because management of data supports *all* drivers and outcomes.

Let's get to the actual creation of a strategy.

Ownership

I cannot stress the importance of this enough. The data strategy and management principles should be owned by someone whose *only* responsibility is data. Assigning it to IT or a particular branch of the business immediately presents conflicts of interest. Yes, everybody should have the same objectives but conflicts always arise and they arise frequently and it needs to be someone's role to "defend" the data. It is not just the conflict of interest that is problematic; it is the authority for both direction and daily operation.

This role, because of these conflicts and authority, needs to report to the highest level in the company. A Chief Data Officer (CDO) that reports to the CEO or the Board is ideal. In some companies the CDO title refers to Chief Digital Officer; they are not the same so do not confuse the two. I am not going to "demand" a specific role or define your reporting structure, but after reading this book I hope you would understand that conflicts of interest and the lack of company-wide authority will undermine the progress, objectives and even the quality of the data. Does your company have a Chief Information Security Officer (CISO)? In many companies they report to the highest levels because they cannot be compromised by other initiatives that might conflict with the security of the company. The security of the information is entirely about data. Is it not odd that the security of the data has a higher priority than the data itself? A CISO is at that level for the same reasons that I expressed about data. There cannot be conflicts of interest and the scope and authority needs to be company-wide. To be clear, data security is one of the aspects of data management. That does not mean that I believe that the CISO should report to the CDO. It does mean that data security is impacted by data management and by the logical approach of data management expressed in this book.

The scope and level of ownership does more than add the correct skills, authority, and scope; it is a visible sign of the company commitment to data. I cannot emphasize the importance of this enough. If people see that the strategy, principles, measurements, and goals apply differently depending on who you are, they will walk away and rightly question the company's commitment to managing data and you will never get the benefit from the efforts.

Where To Start

I stated that a strategy is not just a mission statement but any plan or strategy needs to start with objectives. When I have seen companies attempt data strategies, I usually see end-state terminology rather than data management objectives. The end-state impacts need to be kept in mind but there should be objectives that *enable* those end-states. This book is really about that enablement. The end-state terminologies can also be very buzzword oriented such as, "We are going to be a *data-driven* company". I have yet to see one define how they would do that or even what that means to them. People are left with the buzzwords and will tell you the company is data-driven. I guess that means they use data, so does everybody else and that takes no strategy. Another one is to *democratize* data. I have been told this means that anybody should have access to any data they want at any time for any purpose. I am not sure that all agree with that definition but it is the only one that I have personally heard from inside companies that are using that word. Yet another is *monetizing* data. Some of these words will come up again. Let's take a look at a more simplistic set of management objectives.

Here are the three questions referred to earlier:

1. What data do you have?
2. What does the data mean?
3. Where is the data?

It's hard to imagine that you can do much that is useful with data without knowing these three things. You need these answers for reporting, analytics, security, compliance, etc. These are also three things that sound very logical and it might be assumed that the answers are obvious. The objective is simple, the words are simple, but the answers are certainly not simple due to a lack of data management and the rapid growth of data and technologies. The volume of data and access to data across the world has exploded. Combine that with network speeds and cheap storage and you find that data morphs and proliferates exponentially almost by the minute.

Without digging into the details yet of how that can be managed (and it can be), the first step after assigning the appropriate ownership is an assessment of what you know. What principles or management is in place that enables answers to the three questions? You might be tempted to note the things that hinder the answers to these questions but that list could get very long and it really isn't very productive. The reason I say that it isn't productive is that if the focus is on how to eliminate the hindrance, then the effort is removed from finding the answers to the three questions. Once the answers to the three questions are known, the hindrance is irrelevant.

Here are some general guidelines for assessing what you know in regard to the three questions (Start with broad rather than deep):

- Do you know *all* of the places that data is stored?
- Can you categorize (roll up) data so that the answers are more achievable?
- Where are the places data is documented in any way?
- What types of control are in place regarding data proliferation, or even knowledge of proliferation?
- Do you have any place where the meaning of data is documented?
- How many people (in what roles) are involved in "managing" data. This includes DBAs, security, data governance, infrastructure, storage management, integration, etc.
- What is your total volume of storage space? Include all locations and all devices: network storage, servers, desktops, laptops, cloud, etc.
- This list is not complete. Complete reading this book.

Do you need to have a strategy for all locations and devices and answer the three questions for them? Absolutely. It is possible that different types of data may be managed at different levels, but you still need to be able to "type" the data and know where it is.

Don't expect to find complete answers to any of these questions to begin with, so put the answers in a place where they can easily be updated. And there we have hit upon a key factor in success, the ease of management of metadata. This is metadata; it is not metadata about the details of data elements, but rather data about a broader reflection of the status of your data as a whole.

So far there are three steps toward a data strategy: identify owner, goal of being able to answer three questions, and documenting your current state toward the answers to those questions in a manageable way. Managing to the three questions puts you in a position to be better prepared for the unforeseen. Imagine that you find new uses for combinations of data, or that there are new regulations, or any other business initiative; you *always* need to know the answers to the questions. Again, some will reject this as not being of "business value" to the bottom line. Some will say that I need to create new initiatives with the data and I need to show that it is making money. We might as well address the pushback at a high level right now.

Resistance to a Strategy to Manage Data

I spoke of hindrance to answering the three questions not being a focal point. That should not imply that awareness and preparedness is not essential for the strategy itself. You will never get to the three questions without some level of strategy and attempt to manage data. This section is about some of the resistance that you will see to a strategy that manages data.

The most powerful resistance to a successful strategy to manage data is leadership. If the top leadership of the company is not aligned, your strategy will fail. Why would leadership not be aligned? Because they don't see either the value or the risk. As stated, the importance of the leadership role in managing data is critical, so this is likely not the last time you will hear it. That does not mean that if you do not have buy-in or this leadership structure that the rest of this book is of no value. There is the argument that, "Doing something is better than doing nothing." Depending on the objectives, it may be relatively "very little" more than nothing. It is still a goal to be achieved. Use this book and any resources at your disposal to make the case. Be persistent.

One of the biggest operational hurdles will be the perception that people are losing their freedom with data. This will likely manifest itself as complaints about not being able to do their job. This is one to be prepared for with facts. The data that people need to do their job is likely different than the data that they have been using or have access to. It is also likely that the current method of using the data is not the only way, in fact, it might not be the most productive way for them to do their job. I understand that things do not and cannot change overnight, that is the reason that a strategy is needed. The strategy will involve change, but it is change for the better and will not destroy the needs of the company. It will enable the needs of the company while reducing the company's risk.

Another example of resistance might come when it is determined that something needs to be done about the out of control movement of data. The use of data is reliant upon accurate data and accurate data is dependent on, for one thing, knowing the *appropriate* source. The appropriate source is singular. Every movement of data and every alternative source for data adds significant risk to the data being different and the likelihood of factual data dwindles. We will discuss this concept in detail. For now, the point is that principles, rules, and a measurable strategy around managing various aspects of data are critical.

Steps So Far

I am extending some steps that I considered implied but I want to be explicit:

1. Get leadership buy-in at the highest level
2. Identify a single lead role that is responsible for the data strategy and data management
3. Set the goal of being able to answer three questions

4. Identify roles and responsibilities (Initial roles)
5. Inventory current state of being able to answer the three questions
   a. Inventory current state of roles and tools
   b. Define location of this *high-level* metadata and the process to maintain it
6. Start building a high-level roadmap to success that allows for measurability and tracking and can be updated (probably on a quarterly basis with additional detailed initiatives)
   a. Identify 2-4 initiatives that are broad enough to involve most people and not so deep to cause immediate culture shock. The shock of having an organization and a leader that is responsible for "data" is possibly going to be enough of an initial shock. (This is just a general recommendation. Each situation is different and some may call for a bit heavier initial action if there is the leadership support for it.)

A Little More On The Three Questions

Once you dig into the three questions, you may be surprised at how encompassing those three questions really are and how much they are dependent on each other.

1. What data do you have?
   a. You can certainly *begin* with grouping data that collectively means something. Examples of a grouping of data would be an invoice, an order, contracts, sales, etc.
   b. This can be a significant effort to just get to that level, but be prepared for the levels of information as they come. There will be types of invoices, orders, etc.

  c. The next level after the type is the individual elements within that grouping.

2. What does the data mean?

  a. The meaning follows all of the same levels as the groupings and elements. Yes, you need to define the grouping and types as well as the elements.

3. Where is the data?

  a. As big as the other two are, this one grows rapidly

  b. Where is your *one* authoritative location for any given type of grouping? You can start with this but that does not fully answer the question, however it is a huge start. We will talk about this in detail in the chapters about master data management and integration.

  c. If you only get this far you have made amazing progress that few have clearly defined, but the even bigger complexity comes with answering the question of where else that data resides. Do you even have a way to know?

  d. Even if you do know, can you tie back to the what and meaning because once data is moved to another location, it is very likely different than the original. If it is different in content or meaning, what is it and what does it mean? You have probably just identified a new set of data that loops back to the *what* and the *meaning*.

  e. I did not share this last circular scenario to make it seem impossible, because it is possible, but rather to emphasize that data needs to be managed from the beginning. Once it is out of control, it becomes increasingly out of control and answering three simple questions becomes a "seemingly" insurmountable task.

If you are thinking that your data is already out of control, it is not too late but the more out of control the situation, the more likely it is that people will feel the impacts of getting it in control. Again, it is possible.

Factors for Success
- Make the case for data management (Long story and elevator speech)
- Have the right ownership role at the right level with the right authority
- Have a company-wide scope of data management from the beginning
- Create well-defined roles and responsibilities (in and out of the immediate org.)
- Plan on a layered approach. Add more detail and layers as able
- The whole company does not need to advance at the same speed once started, but everyone is measured. (In other words, don't hold up others because of some that are behind.)
- Time – Have high expectations but do not expect everything to happen at once
- Some of the strategy will likely contain "rules" just like managing security has rules. Failure to follow the rules must have consequences or the rules are not really rules.
- Do not tie applications, people, or departments to data. Data is managed as data regardless of application usage or creation. Just like other business assets, they are not "owned" by a department, person, or application; they are owned by the company. Applications change, technologies change, org structures change and people change; none of those changes has any impact on the data.

- Another key aspect to a successful strategy is to understand the current culture and processes that are in place. There are often opportunities to "plug in" to current processes or at least not destroy them in order to make the management process less disruptive. It will also be important to identify key metrics that highlight the progress both from a data management perspective and a business value perspective.

- Communication. Keep people involved and set clear expectations. Do not make promises, rules, or demands that have not been fully defined such that they can be measured.

- Read this book. There are details of implementation methods and principles that should prove useful.

I want to add a couple more thoughts that really do not fit into bullet points before wrapping up the strategy concept chapter.

Even if you have a CDO-type role, I understand that a CDO is not only going to be solely about managing data. Initiatives will move forward for using data, assisted by the CDO, prior to data management being in place. This is not abandoning a strategy; it puts more emphasis on the already strong case for a strategy to manage data. Even without "managing" data in the short-term, all effort should be made to help ensure that the situation is not made worse by short-term goals and allowing things to get even more out of control. It should be noted that the word control is going to be a trigger word for many. In response to a negative reaction to control, I want to step back to the simple concept of data being an asset. Conceptually make it as simple as money. Do you not put money in a safe place? Do you not control who can spend it? Is it not a crime to make copies (forgery) of money? There are so many analogies. I am not saying that the treatment of data is identical to money, but it is probably closer than where you are today.

If you have the answers to the three questions, you are in a strong position for reliable use of the data. Reliable or not, it will be used. Part of the strategy is to make it more reliable and get it moving toward fact. Speaking of fact, how do you show compliance to regulations and laws, produce data under subpoena, or use data as a legal defense without it being facts? The situation today is that people get away with it, but as soon as attorneys (including attorneys general) and judges wise up to the requirements of factual data and the way that data is managed (or not managed), the tide will change. Will you be ready? The days of saying, "this is the best that we can do and doing anything better is unreasonable" will be over. Facts are possible. "Good enough" will not always be acceptable.

The scope of the strategy is important as well. In this case I do not mean the company-wide scope. I mean the type of functions that are covered by the strategy. Anything that falls within the broad scope of data management should be included in the strategy in some form. This does not mean that the reporting structure of all roles report into the CDO-type role. There are many ways to slice the reporting structure, but the ownership of the management requirements of data should be clear. I keep referencing security because security is a much more established concept in most companies so it is a good reference. Security would not usually own application development but they would usually provide requirements with some level of accountability and measurement. The same is true for infrastructure, databases, networks and even personal computer security. There is at least one group that should be direct reporting in this org and that is the leadership for data governance. We will discuss this in detail in the data governance chapter.

Details of strategies with a logical approach are contained in the rest of this book.

Chapter 3

DATA CAPTURE

We have talked about the importance of managing data from the "beginning" and the beginning is data capture. This is where the initial requirements need to be met. Remember this?

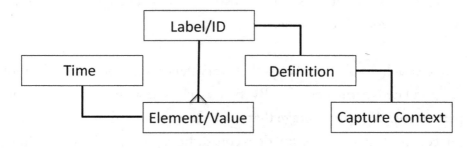

Figure 3-1

There must be minimal metadata regarding the value that includes a label, context, time, and a meaning (definition). The definition can arguably be set in detail later but basic definition is required. There is no valid place to capture the value, the time, and the context other than at the point of capture. We should probably clarify what is meant by the *point of capture*. It is fairly simple; it is the first place where the data exists within your control.

The majority of the time, but not always, it is going to be an application that is within your control that captures or creates the data. Creating and capturing, for the purpose of this discussion, are both valid scenarios of data capture. This point within the application is the first place where data can wander off the data management path. The application has accountability for the data's metadata and for the integrity of the data within the application.

At this point I want to explain a little more about the possible capture scenarios:

1. Most often an application (code) is the first touch point and the process will include the first persistence of the data.
2. It is also possible that the first touch point is persistent data or data from a source outside of your control.
3. It is possible that the application will touch (capture) the data and never persist it. This is the least likely and should be avoided if possible.

I should probably clarify that persistence has some expectation of "regulated permanence". By that I mean that persistence is not permanent. Memory storage that can be lost or flushed on failures does not constitute persistence, but does constitute capture for this discussion. Let's look at a little more detail around each scenario:

1. The first scenario on the list is the most common and will receive the most time for the rest of this chapter. This scenario is when your application/code has control of the data creation and its meaning. The application is responsible

for the metadata because it is in control of the label, context, time, and manipulations that can change the meaning.

2. The "initial persistence of data" scenario would exist where, for example, you have an FTP site and people are allowed to "put" data to this FTP server. I am not making this technology specific, but this works as an example because of the *point of capture* definition stating "within your control". The first place where you control the data is after it is persisted on the FTP server. You may control access to the server, but someone else is controlling the data. In addition, the nature of FTP, especially secure FTP, ensures the completeness of the data. I don't want to spend too much time on the technology aspect of this but realize that when you are touching the data on the FTP server, you are touching it to do something with it other than capture it and it already needs to contain the required attribution (metadata) to make the data "real". Whoever provided the data needs to tell you the label, definition, time, and context of capture because they owned the initial capture context and attribution. If they don't, you will be making stuff up or documenting your receipt of the data as the time and context, which can be useful but it is a different set of data. Picking data up from another company is similar when it comes to metadata. This is more of a hybrid scenario (combining scenarios 1 and 2) because your application picking it up still has the ability to manipulate the data. However, the initial metadata needs to come with the data you are picking up from company x or you, again, would be in a situation of making stuff up. A simple example is if you receive an invoice from company x, you need to know what each element is named, what it means, and when it was created (which might be one of the elements), and the context

is the fact that it was an invoice provided via company x.

This is a good point to talk about assumptions and accuracy of metadata. It would not be uncommon for someone to make a statement that this is the data captured by company x that provided you the data. Unless you have statements and metadata to that effect, the accurate context and time is that it is the data that you received from company x; in some cases that can be a very important distinction. You do not own or probably even have knowledge of how or when company x processed the data before sending it to you unless they send metadata with the data.

3. Avoid if possible. Let's use my example of a retailer that wanted to scan my driver's license for the purpose of purchasing a video game. Let's say that they were being responsible with my driver's license data and just using it to validate my age. One data flow could be that they "capture" all of the information from my DL. While sitting in the application, they pull out the age and verify that it meets the age qualification and then discard all of the data from the DL and only persist the indicator that the age was verified with a DL. They truly did capture all of the data and at that point had some accountability for what is done with it. This also brings up a good point of *detail* pertinent to more than just this scenario.

The requirements for all of the metadata still exists, but the scenarios and types of data can impact how and at what level the metadata is stored.

There are two basic requirements for the metadata:

1. When the data is moved the metadata *must* remain associated with the data
2. All data requires metadata

In many situations each data element will have metadata associated directly with each element. The next level up from that allows for metadata to be associated with multiple elements. This is not uncommon and there are multiple technical ways to accomplish this, keeping in mind that the first requirement above still applies. When multiple data elements carry *identical* metadata the metadata can be stored at a higher level. The data scanned from a driver's license or credit card or the information that a customer entered on a form all have the same context metadata. In those cases the time is likely also the same across all of them but would not have to be in the case of a form where the data is captured on each element of the form rather than at completion of the form. At a higher aggregate level, which is *very* rare, is the grouping of the elements themselves. The example of the driver's license scan would be one where you may not even know all of the elements that are captured. As I said, this is very rare and it would be much better and safer to never capture any data that is not needed rather than capturing it and throwing it away. Doing the latter exposes you to more risk and liability if anyone were to make a mistake or even accuse you of making a mistake. The statement, "I never captured it", is far stronger than "I captured it but I didn't use it".

In this rare case, the expectation is that the data never flows anywhere so the first requirement is irrelevant. However, when asked, the information about the data and its disposition needs to be available.

All data, outside of this rare exception, must have the metadata or the explicit reference to the metadata flow with it from beginning to end. The end is when the data is permanently destroyed. Typical data capture to destruction, in all of its iterations, replications, and movements is typically a very long and complex road and we will define ways to simplify it in the chapters on integration and methodology. For now, we will try to stick to the data capture process.

The data capture process includes the persistence of the data, but the first persistence of the data contained within the data capture process may or may not be the *one authoritative source* for this data. If required, further movement beyond the initial persistence to the one authoritative source will offer more risk of variation. Variation can include manipulation, filters, formatting, as well as unintentionally dropped data. I do not want to go too deep into the one authoritative source yet, but I do want to make a few very important points that can relate to the data capture process:

1. The first place that the data is stored may not be the one authoritative source for the data.

2. As stated previously, data movement adds risk but it is more than data movement; it is every time and every place where the data is "touched". How much data manipulation is done within the application or storage processes, or more precisely *any code*? During the capture process, how many times is data touched prior to its initial storage? Manipulation of data within code is one of the easiest ways to *lose* the meaning of the data and to lose control.

3. The application does not "own" the data. This will come up in other aspects, but the consistent message is that if there is a perception that a single application owns the data, then the data is for a single purpose rather than for any purpose and the integrity of the data suffers.

Let's take a look at a potential data capture process. There are many possibilities, so this is just an example that it may not be a *single* "raw data" step when completing an online form.

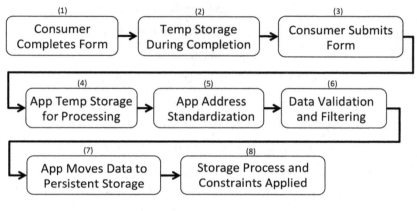

Figure 3-2

I know the diagram is not in a standard workflow format, but the purpose of the diagram is for *all* to understand the concept that capture can be more than one step. This data flow is likely not what you are doing, at least I hope not, but the point of the flow is that many things can happen and it is not unusual for some of them to happen. At the end of this data capture process, all of the data can no longer be stated as data captured from the consumer. Any step that modifies data owns updates to the metadata. This rarely happens; after all, the steps are just intended to make the data more consistent, more useable, and stop systems from breaking. Those justifications are likely avoidable but regardless of the reason or justification, the data is still modified.

This is not a class in application development but consider some of the steps in Figure 3-2 and what might happen to the data:

1. There is no problem with a form in itself

2. Temp storage is not an issue as long as it is in sync with what the consumer sees on the form; if the data in the temp storage is wiped, so is the data on the form

3. No issue with submitting the form as along as the successful submission is tied to any remaining steps and any changes or failures are presented back to the consumer for acceptance

4. Assume temp storage has no constraints and will accept all entered data regardless of type or size or that failures are reported to and accepted by the consumer

5. Address standardization will change some data and unless the consumer approves, this is no longer consumer entered data

6. Confirming valid values across data fields that would be incompatible such as conflicting dates; this could also be formatting or truncating entries

7. Application moving data needs to have the accountability for completeness and integrity of data and mechanisms to respond to failures, otherwise dropped data can occur

8. Processing data into persistent storage can vary greatly across technologies and designs but imagine there is a designed or technical constraint on the storage that does not allow certain lengths of data or certain characters

Some of these that could be issues would clearly be poor design but poor designs happen and who is testing, making decisions, or even stating the requirements related to the metadata and integrity of the data? A couple of design considerations in this poor example can address all of the concerns. If you are expecting to be able to state that this information came from the consumer, the consumer needs to enter or approve all changes and submission does not complete until they do. There should be no constraints on the data repository beyond what might be represented in the form itself. For example, if the repository is designed for a field size of 50 characters, it is fine as long as the form does not allow more. The same would be true for special characters or extended character sets. The safe bet is no constraints on the first persistent storage because, over time, the people responsible for maintaining the repository and the application are likely different people and are not likely to maintain ongoing validation across roles.

Another approach to this would be to take the form data directly to the unconstrained repository and make any modifications after persisting the data. You then have both data sets with different metadata but you know what you have. I am not here to tell you what is right for your situation but rather to point out the responsibility for the data integrity, including its metadata. This also starts to identify that it is not just one role or process that is responsible. Any role or process that touches data has a responsibility for its integrity and metadata. We will get more into that concept as the data moves beyond its initial repository and even beyond the one authoritative source.

Data capture and this entire book is not about a particular technology or implementation pattern; it is about logical requirements. I will occasionally provide examples of technology-based solutions, but do not write them off as being a technology that you do not use or you will miss the point. There are hundreds of ways to solve for a given problem and likewise to meet the requirements of managing data.

We have stepped through a few potential failures in the integrity of the data within the data capture process and hopefully you have none of them. How do you know? I come back to the questions of who is setting the requirements and who is making the decisions. In many cases, it is the developer that is making decisions for the purpose as they understand it. The lack of errors and validating functionality are most often at the forefront, and the integrity of the metadata is not likely to be a major (or even minor) consideration even though the benefits are far reaching and resolve a number of design and functional failures. The focus on data is a culture shift that takes time and requires ownership.

Chapter 4

DATA PRIVACY

It is inevitable that through the discussion of data privacy we will talk about laws regarding data privacy. Privacy laws, for many, are driving the "concern" for data privacy and will eventually have a beneficial impact on general data management. It is also likely that through this discussion the concept of ethics will come up. Ethical is such a subjective term that it can be used and manipulated in any way a person or business determines is appropriate to them. Privacy is a complex and ever-changing topic that cannot be covered in detail in one chapter. There are organizations that focus on privacy and one is the International Association of Privacy Professionals (IAPP) that you can find at IAPP.org. The purpose of this chapter in this book is to set the context of its relevance to a logical approach to data management.

There are a number of ways to slice the subject of data privacy but let's start with the social aspect of data and how it drives or hinders data privacy.

Socially Shared Information

The way society looks at data privacy has changed a great deal over time. You could conclude that the advent of social media and general Internet usage has made many people (especially younger people) much more willing to share information. For some, it is just a growing acceptance of, "That's just the way it works." Many click through acceptance of privacy policies without giving it a thought and agree to things that they have no idea they are agreeing to. You could say that is on them, but then again it seems to not only be allowed but encouraged, and in some cases is required for doing business with a company or accessing their website.

This section on shared information is about the information many would think to be "private" and yet is freely "shared". This term of sharing is merely allowing anyone access to a person's information. By anyone, I do not mean the intent was to share with everyone. This is posting your name or birthday, making comments about an event, posting a picture of where you are, sending a text or email, and all of the information that is not thought about by many as *sharing* their data. I don't want to go too deep into that information, but understand that any information about you qualifies as personal information. The fact that you are on vacation and where you are can have unexpected and unwanted results when shared with the world; you have to assume that once you share it, you can *never* take it back.

The personal information that you share, whether intentional or otherwise, has the opportunity to both help you and hurt you. Is the power of what is good or bad for you a decision that should be handed over to a company with which you are doing some form of business or just happened to cross their path? This is starting to border on both ethics and the law. There are some laws that answer that question for some data in some locations. The ethical use of personal data is something that an individual needs to take some responsibility for. Based on the nature of things, I would suggest not relying on any company, whose purpose for having your data is to make money, to make what you would consider ethical decisions or decisions in your best interest.

The subject of this section is the social aspect and so far we have talked about the sharing of data from the person perspective. I started with this perspective because ultimately it is the person that should be accountable for the information about themselves, but that is not reality. In many cases, the person freely offers information and believes that they have the ability to control that data including pulling it back if they change their mind. This expectation, in most cases, is not accounted for by the companies accepting their data. There is a cost to the company to allow for a person to be able to permanently remove data they have offered. It may seem like a reasonable expectation to the person, but it comes with a cost and what is the benefit to the company? Depending on how the data has been managed, it could have a fairly significant cost to the company with very little value other than meeting a person's request or potentially complying with more laws in the future. It is likely far less costly to give the person the impression that their data is removed and not show it to them anymore, but it does not mean that the data is "removed" and not being used for other purposes.

Collected Data

We have been primarily talking about data that people share about themselves. There is also the information that can be associated with a person that is not provided directly by the person but is captured in large volumes. The variety of ways that it can be captured, the technologies that enable capture, the low cost of mass volumes of storage, and the advent of advanced analytics, including machine learning and artificial intelligence, has led companies to capture masses of data. In many cases having no idea how or if they will use some of it, and in some cases not even knowing what it is. I hope it is obvious that could be a problem?

This falls under the realm of "social" because a significant amount of this data is collected via social Internet and device mechanisms. This includes your company's website in this social concept. This is not exclusive to social media, even though that has expanded the exposure significantly; the social aspect in this regard refers more to social norms. One might think that sharing and collecting personal data has expanded in its social acceptance and it certainly has in volume, but that does not mean that previous practices were secure or that the Internet is the only way of collecting data. Here are a couple of personal examples:

- It was just within the last year that I went to a new dentist office and they asked me for my social security number. When I asked why they wanted it, they said that it was what they used as their patient ID. There are laws that restrict this type of use of a social security number but they either didn't know or didn't care. They had likely been doing it without a thought since they started the practice and by their reaction, in fact they stated so, I was the first patient to object. They were not going to treat me. They did after I raised my objection to a higher level. Sharing my information with them that they did not need certainly did me no good, it really did them no good, and it raised their risk and liability of exposing their clients' PII (Personally Identifiable Information). So why? Is "because" a good answer? They found it convenient, while creating their own unique ID would have served their purpose just as well. You might think this practice is restricted to only very small operations −not so.

- I also recently went into a major retailer to buy an Xbox game. The game was rated MA and they asked to scan my driver's license. Now I am gray haired and in my 60's with obvious wrinkles showing my age, but I could not buy a video game without allowing them to access all of the information that is obtained from the scan of my driver's license. I have no idea what they collect or keep, but by handing it to them it could be implied that I gave them permission to collect all of the data. This happened twice and one time the manager did an override and the other I left without the purchase. I never attempted future purchases in that store. I will tell you that people looked at me like I was a real jerk and I could see the thoughts, "Just give them your damn driver's license". This is the societal aspect. Businesses will do what they can to collect data as long as society and laws do not prevent them. Is this right? We will get to the ethical question, but it is certainly not wrong in the sense of being illegal (yet).

How much data are you collecting because you can? Do you need it? Is it in the best interest of your company? Is there another way? It is evident that there is no end in sight for the increase in collection of more and more data in more and more ways. The sheer volume of data increases the challenge and risk to not only the person having their data collected but to the companies needing to "manage" that volume of data. I have no way to be sure what direction the social acceptance and the legal regulations will take in the next few years and decades, but the purpose of this book is to be prepared regardless of direction.

Sharing / Buying / Selling

One aspect of PI (Personal Information) data, that may start with social norms but is an adjacent impact, is the sharing and selling of data. There are companies whose primary business is to broker and match information about people. Some is benign demographic data until it is matched to a specific person. If your company is buying or sharing this data, there is a good chance that you are aware of it, but it is more data with a different context and is another type of data to be managed.

A company collecting data and sharing it is not inherently bad; it can benefit the end-users and certainly can benefit the company. It does need to be recognized that PI data is a different type of data that can cause issues for the person as well as the company. The issues that sharing and receiving data can cause for the company are likely to increase with more laws and regulations specific to selling data, which can impact the recipients of the data as well.

Once data is transferred across companies, the traceability and retrievability today is pretty much non-existent. Also keep in mind that the reliability and accuracy of data diminishes with every share. Data from an outside source should *not* be considered as fact unless it is the authoritative source and the integration is monitored and managed (more on that later). An example of an external authority source might be the mover's list from the United States Postal Service. This would not replace the facts provided by a person, but it would be a fact that a person has notified the US government that they are moving or have moved. Regardless of where the data is sourced, PI data is the responsibility of any company that has it. Laws and litigation will drive the accountability.

Categories of Personal Data

We have been talking about people being freer with personal data. This is not a new concept but it is certainly increasing. This is a good place to further discuss the two primary categories of personal data. They are very relevant to laws and therefore relevant to data management. The two primary categories are PII and PI. There is information referred to as PII (Personally Identifiable Information). There is also PI (Personal Information) data. You will find, however, that not all laws are consistent in the use of the terms even though they reference the need to distinguish two definitions. For your sake, it is important to distinguish the difference between these two categories.

Examples of PII data include elements that allow someone to identify *you* such as driver's license, social security number, some combinations of name address, address and phone number, etc. These are the data elements that singularly or in combination allow you to identify a unique person. There are requirements specific to PII and there has been even more of a focus due to the increase in identity theft. These data elements enable that theft.

PI information generally contains PII plus *all* of the information that is or can be attached to an identified person. The term "can be" is an important distinction when we get to laws and management. This includes many things but a few examples would be things that you have purchased, your Internet usage, income, age, relatives, friends, where you have been, emails, texts, devices that you have and when you use them, every click you have made on the Internet and everything you have, etc. The list is much, much longer and now includes many things that just a couple years ago might have been unimaginable. Imagine what the future holds. Some data is certainly more sensitive and there are specifically different laws related to different data.

Essentially *anything* that can potentially be tied back to a person can fall in that PI category. It is not the simple concept anymore of my name, address, phone number, email, social security number, driver's license number, etc. but consider your conversations (in any form), where you went, what you did, how you spend your money, how you use the Internet, crimes you have committed or even thought about. Yes, what you thought about. Analysis of information identifies you with the likelihood to do things, say things, buy things, look at things, and can identify your position on religion, abortion, sex, politics, etc. But you didn't search the Internet for anything that you wouldn't want someone to know and nobody can certainly monitor your thoughts. Can they? The point is that true or not, the information derived about you by any company is included in PI data.

This brings me to one of the advancements that is experiencing exponential growth. Technology. Think about what is visible outwardly either by visible or monitored indicators. Where you went, where you stopped, where you looked, where your eyes focused, when you turned your head, when you slowed your pace, when your heart rate went up or down, how you slept, what you ate, or when you used what devices.

In addition to the distinction between PII and PI data, there are a couple more "slices" of this same data that will be relevant to management of PI data. Those two categories are how the data was collected/created and what it is used for. This more relevant detail, but generally the method used for collection ties directly to data capture, so attaching metadata at the time of capture is a logical addition to data capture. It could even be argued that the method of capture is already included in the data context metadata, but it is important enough with PI to call it out. The usage "slice" of the data is a whole different concept that may not be metadata attached to the data itself, but does relate to data management, the data usage, and the data proliferation.

Laws and Regulations

As stated, there is no way to know for sure what direction things will take regarding laws impacting data privacy, but I can provide a brief synopsis of the history and some current trends. Laws in the United States regarding privacy began early in the country's existence. There was the Fourth Amendment in the Bill of Rights that mentioned "papers" as property of a person and there was a law passed a few years later specifically regarding the opening of mail. Some of the early laws were pointed toward the *government* accessing information, but the scope of access and purpose has evolved over the years.

Laws, torts, and legal precedents related to how information can be acquired in matters of criminal investigations and civil litigation have also been around for some time. Laws regarding recording a conversation have also been a factor in various ways across states for some time.

Laws related to information have been growing throughout the seventeen, eighteen, and nineteen hundreds. Many of them were related to communications such as mail and telegraphs. Generalities related to papers, "information", and data grew as well. The line between data, information, papers, property, and even identity has been debated as part of this evolution and litigation. As the line blurs between them, let's assume that the medium of information is irrelevant. As with the logical approach to data management not being dependent on technologies, the medium of information "should be" irrelevant to the definition and laws regarding privacy. Some may debate that, but this is not the place for that and you want to be prepared even if it changes. I believe that there is already a pattern starting to show that rather than the storage medium, the relevant factor is the function. What was the intended function and intended audience of the information? Hence, the term "private".

You might think that the information about you that is covered by laws such as HIPAA is a newer concept, but information collected about you through the census grew in volume through the 1800s and was finally regulated by congress in 1919. The recognition of more explicit regulations started coming about with a variety of laws around the world. Here is a very small sampling of some of the laws related to privacy:

- 1778 – The Fourth Amendment related to "illegal search and seizure".
- 1782 – Congress passed a law that mail should not be opened.
- 1800s (mid) – The number of personal questions in the census was rapidly increasing and the answers were publicly posted.

- 1877 – Supreme Court upheld that the Fourth Amendment applied to letters and specified that it applied to a person's "papers".
- 1880 – New protection for telegrams.
- 1800s (late) – The development of more readily available small camera and increased newspaper distribution led to more litigation. Consideration started to be given for the intent of the "property" and added the concept of "being left alone".
- 1900s (early) – The concept of "consent" starts to be more prevalent.
- 1900s (mid) – The concept of "public vs. private" information evolves.
- 1960s – Court ruling roughly states that information that a person exposes to the public is not covered by the Fourth Amendment, but information that was intended to be private (even if it is accessible to the public) is covered by the Fourth Amendment.
- 1974 – Privacy Act establishes a code of information practices that governs the information about individuals that is maintained in systems of records by federal agencies.
- 1996 - The Health Insurance Portability and Accountability Act (HIPAA). While this involves privacy, it is not its sole or even initial purpose. The title alone should tell you that.
- 2018 – General Data Protection Regulation (GDPR) is a law in the EU but has more broad reaching impacts.
- 2020 – California Consumer Privacy Act (CCPA) has a number of high-level similarities to GDPR and is specific to the residents of California. Many more states have privacy laws in the works.

This is a very light sampling of laws and rulings from a list of hundreds or thousands. As you can see from this sampling, some of the laws regarding personal data have been on the books for quite some time, but they are changing and expanding for good reason. The type of technologies involved with data has expanded and any laws written specific to technology are left in the dust or open to arguments of relevance. The volume of data and awareness of potential consequences have had, and may continue to have, an impact on new laws. Early reference to privacy was more about invasion of privacy in general and by the government, but the data privacy laws have started being more pervasive since the 1990s.

While there has been an evolution of technologies and laws, there are some common themes and trends among the vast majority of laws across the entire timeline. There is a great deal of relevance applied to the method of collection, the intended purpose of the information, and a growing clarity on the "permission" to access.

Let's look at a little bit more detail of the more recent regulations.

HIPAA – The Health Insurance Portability and Accountability Act. A major function of this law is to provide a mechanism for sharing personal health information (PHI) across providers such as clinics and insurance companies. It also has allowances for 12 reasons that the information can be shared without approval when in the best interest of the public. PHI is a subset of PI and carries similar characteristics, in that it must be associated with PII data to be considered PHI. Many people see this as a privacy law and it does cover the requirements of approval but *only for the "covered entities"* such as the providers of health care and insurance companies that meet certain criteria. It has a great deal of visibility because most people are exposed via the requirement of the providers to share the HIPAA rules. You may see them when you are in the emergency room or visiting a new clinic. People have heard the term and most likely have a misperception of what rights they have and what it actually protects. HIPAA, while driven by enabling standards for sharing data, acknowledges the potential impact of technology advancements on the privacy of data across systems and companies.

GDPR – General Data Protection Regulation. The scope of GDPR being limited to the EU has reaches beyond the EU in that it included people residing in the EU regardless of where they do business as well as companies having a "presence" in the EU. This is the first major law starting to define the rights people have related to their personal data for the entire life of the data. It puts measurable expectations on companies handling personal data and outlines the requirements and penalties regarding those expectations. I am not going to try to convey the totality of 88 pages plus the accompanying directives of GDPR. The regulation declares, "The protection of natural persons in relation to the processing of personal data is a fundamental right."

In addition to the principles, the person's rights are laid out in detail and include:
- The right to access their data
- The right to correct their data
- The right to have their data removed
- The right to restrict the use of their data
- The right to transfer their data

There is a prominence of approval for usage and transparency in the specifics of the use. The regulation is all-inclusive in its definition of the scope of data as being any data that can be related to an identified or identifiable person. This a very brief summary and obviously there is a lot more to GDPR, but the idea of a person's right to their data is quite clear in the intent and extends to the life of the data.

CCPA - California Consumer Protection Act is one of the more recent laws. Other states have similar (but different) laws in the works. They are similar in concept and in a number of specifics to GDPR. Its focus is on defining the rights of a person, within scope, related to the "control" of information about them. A very brief summary of this requires that the business needs to respond to a request from a consumer to share with them what data they have collected about them and from where. The consumer also has the right to request that data be removed from the company's records with some exceptions that are essential to the operations of the company. This short synopsis is very over-simplified but take a moment to consider this. *All data* that *can be* associated with that person in any way. Everything they have purchased, ordered, looked at, asked about, where they have been, their height, weight and age, etc. The etcetera is bigger than you may think in many companies.

The three questions are core to the ability to respond to this request. You have to know what you have (associated with a person), what it means (and is used for), the context of its collection, and *all* of the places that it resides. Oh yes, combine the what it is used for with the where it is because all instances of the data may not be required for business operations. Companies will respond and some will make gallant efforts to do the best that they can, but who can truthfully answer all of those questions? Now add the fact that at least 10 other states are talking about similar but different laws and the burden on companies that are not prepared will be very heavy. The argument that the burden is too heavy will only hold water for so long. Companies will likely find themselves looking for a universal law at the federal level to help ease the pain, but who knows when or if that will happen. The way the states will enforce the laws will vary as well and there may very well be leeway to begin with. I would not bet on that lasting. This is another good example of where using a single driver, such as CCPA, to manage data will not necessarily work for the next law. You need the answers in a complete and methodical way and you need the ability to have controls and measurements in place that enable the appropriate use of data.

The specifics related to the individual laws may have already changed or they may change in the future and that is really not all that important to the purpose of this book. There is enough commonality in these three examples to give evidence of the value of the three questions, the respect for data, and managing its use. This is not a bad way to sum up what data management is. There is actually no way to address laws without being able to answer the three questions. Adding the respect (security and integrity) and the usage of the data encompasses the principles of the laws as well as the scope of data management.

While data management alone will not address all of the implementation requirements of the laws, such as the method for requests to be processed, it is the logical requirement for the actual data portion of the laws. The process requirements within the laws may differ and there are likely ways to find commonality in those, but that portion is not addressed in this book because it is not data management.

The laws have grown and in some cases become more specific, but businesses have been able to move through those changes without turning their internal processes upside-down. So, what might be changing? The vast majority of the laws up until very recently have been about government or people "taking" something from you. We have entered an age of data that arguably defies the previous paradigm. Much of the data that we have talked about in this chapter is data that a person has offered or given "permission" for someone to take. If that is true, what is the issue? There is this concept that a person "sharing" information still owns their data rather than assigning all rights to the business that they allowed to use it and they can change their mind.

While there are commonalities, there are a couple of emerging concepts that are worth calling out. One of those concepts relates to the volume of data but is specific to the scope of the data not just the volume. With the volume of data, the information that *can be* attached to a person is growing thereby increasing the scope of PI data.

The other concept relates to the permission given for access and using data and the creative ways it is being addressed. There have been laws detailing both the intent of the person giving permission and the method that they gave the permission. An example would be the concept of not accepting an "opt-out" but rather requiring an "opt-in". This shifts the assumption in favor of the person rather than the company. There have also been very creative ways of addressing the permission that almost "hides" the approval from the person giving approval. You know those annoying pop-ups that you need to close before continuing. Based on the patterns in the laws, that is likely to have additional clarity and expectations set. The good aspect of this observation is that the method of management is the same; metadata.

We could go on and on about various laws but I hope that you get the picture. There are indicators of what direction laws "might" go, but there are no absolutes; there will be a variety and they will change. So far, to date, I would say that the enforcement of the laws has been light. The crimes or penalties allowed have, in many cases, not been levied to the full extent of the law. I would not bet your company resources that it will stay that way. As has been stated previously, attorneys and judges are likely to improve in their knowledge of what can be done, what is reasonable, and what will be expected. Again, this book is not about the laws, but rather how to be best prepared by managing your data regardless of which way the wind blows.

Data Classification

Throughout this chapter the focus has been on PII and PI data. There is another topic related to privacy and that is your company's or another company's data. Some of that data is intended to be "private". There are even laws around some of that data as well. Financial information, initiatives, or product information that might be used related to insider trading, or corporate espionage have very specific laws related to the use of and access to that data. I am not saying that company data is the same as personal data because it is not, but there are some similarities and overlaps in implementation.

These are generally handled with the concept of data classifications. Of course, classifications can apply to PII and PI data as well. As with other metadata, a data classification can be applied at various levels. It can be specific elements or at a type of data that is well-defined. Classifications will have an impact on the multiple roles and their handling of data. For example, data of a certain classification may have specific access control methods applied, it may require that the data is encrypted, and many other aspects of the operations of data management. As we look at specific implementation details and methods of management, data classifications become one of the ways to determine criteria and measure the company against the objectives.

Ethics

If you think that companies are ethical with the use of personal data, think again. First of all, ethical is such a subjective term that there will be extreme variations in the criteria to be considered ethical. In addition, I believe that most companies have no idea where all of the personal data is located. They collect it, they use some of it, and the way they use it in many cases goes unchecked. What a person might think of as ethical is going to need to be driven by the people that own the data and by the laws. I am not passing moral judgment on companies; it is a reality and an understandable one. It is not something that companies would state out loud or in the fashion that I just did because it doesn't sound that "nice", but this book is based on a logical approach, so it is only logical that companies will maximize the use of any data that they can legally get their hands on. They will also listen to societal and legal pressures that are perceived to impact their bottom line.

The basics of protection in the sense of encryption are in fairly decent shape in many companies. It is a mechanism that is understood and there are technical solutions that have little effect on standard operations. And yet, from total security solutions, there could be holes big enough, as some would say, to drive a Mac truck through. In most cases these are not the technical security issues, although some may exist; they are hiding in plain sight. Some examples include unnecessary internal exposure, unnecessary replication, sharing of data without tracking, and data retention that never ends.

Nobody should be surprised that companies are in business to make money. They also understand that perception is more important than reality to many. Some will say that they are ethical, that they are responsible with data, and that they have robust data management and governance processes because they know those things sound good and they *should* be doing them. Most would show otherwise when faced with some basic questions. Take the three questions for example; can anybody truthfully make these statements regarding their handling of data if they cannot answer the three questions? No!

Again, this is not a matter of legality and it should be expected that companies will use any legal means to know as much as they can about the people that give them money (customers, clients). Of course they will. Is it ethical to let the shareholders down? Companies will justify almost anything that is legal and potentially, in some cases, things that are not.

I am not trying to make the point that all businesses, or even most businesses, will practice unethical activities but rather that ethics will almost always take a backseat to the bottom line and that is okay from the data management perspective. Since "ethical" is a very subjective term, the execution of ethics should really be left out of the data management discussion. It is more appropriate to turn data management justification toward financial benefits and there are many.

Data itself has no soul. Having no soul does not mean that data is bad. It does mean that data itself has no emotion, no intent, no bias, no purpose or sense of right and wrong, and is neither ethical nor unethical. It is of no benefit to the data to indulge in rhetoric related to its ethical use. Honest, factual, and respectful treatment of data is what serves it and those that use it well. Don't pretend; be prepared. This data management approach is logical and the reality of the state of ethics is beneficial to acknowledge in the creation of a logical approach.

Managing PI and PII Data

Now that we have covered the concept of privacy from its social nature, categories of personal information, ethics, and the fact of ever-evolving privacy laws, let's get to the impact on data management if it is not obvious. We have talked about the ability to be prepared for the unknown, and the changing laws certainly fall in that category.

We have talked about various aspects of privacy and some commonalities across them as well as unique aspects of PI data compared to the rest of your data. Where the data comes from, the risks and laws related to the data, and how the data is treated are (or should be) unique to this type of data. There is certainly company confidential data that we just talked about and that is yet another type of data with some similarities in treatment. The three questions are *still* primary across *all* data including the PI, PII, and company confidential data.

Along with the confidential data, we referenced data classifications. Data classifications are one of those things that can be somewhat of a moving target, meaning the data that is in a particular classification can change. Because of this, maintaining the classification as part of metadata attached to the data is probably not the best solution. Maintaining a reference between the metadata and the classification is a better solution. In order for this to work, you obviously need the appropriate metadata that has already been discussed and the data classifications. A couple sample data classifications might include confidential, internal, and public; each carries their own handling requirements.

In addition to the three questions, here are some high level principles for managing this type of data:

1. Make sure that the method of collection is added to the metadata. This can be included in the context metadata or separately, but it will be critical to be prepared for compliance to current and future laws. Was the data provided directly by the person and, if so, how? Was the data collected from them with their permission (such as cookies, location data, device data, interaction data, etc.)? Was the data created through some form of analysis to create a conclusion or set of probabilities? Was the data purchased? And so on…

2. Limit the amount of data. A good starting point is not to collect and store data for which you have no known purpose. It is obviously less data to account for and manage and instantly reduces the liability.

3. Don't keep the data longer than is needed

4. Consider anonymizing the PII data, which makes the previous PI data no longer PI

5. Limit the use, replication, and access. (These are all related to replication)

6. Know the purpose(s) of the data. The unchecked replication of data makes this a much more difficult task. There is an entire chapter on integration and we will discuss more there.

7. Apply the appropriate security. This falls under respecting data. This may seem obvious, but the "proof" of plan and execution will likely be especially helpful for this type of data. There are currently specific requirements for some data; applying it to more data should be considered and planned because this also speaks well to the integrity of the data.

These are mostly data management principles, regardless of the type of data, with only a few specifics identified for this type of data. Most do not see it that way and the new laws seem, to many, to be quite a burden.

The bullet regarding limiting data triggers a few points worth further discussion. The phrase "longer than is needed" was used. Under the guise of advanced analytics, machine learning, and artificial intelligence, there are data hoarders out there that believe "all data is needed". You can never have too much data. This is a questionable approach for a few reasons:

1. More data, more risk, more cost.

2. Data ages and its relevance diminishes.

3. The value of detailed and highly risky data such as PII should have its value challenged. For example, do you need to identify a specific person in order to know that there is a person with patterns that impact your business? In most cases, no. Anonymizing the PII data, especially for reporting and analytics, is a very viable option to consider.

4. Isolate the location of data that is PII or can be PII. Any data that is out of control causes data management problems, but

the PII data attaches itself to all of the PI data every place it goes.

Here is an example of a specific set of data that has some of these principles applied. Credit card data has only been lightly mentioned, but there are standards around the management of credit card data called PCI (Payment Card Industry). There are some pretty standard ways of handling credit card data and methods that are in place so that the company using it does not store the complete credit card data and the data is protected while processing. Some will outsource the complete transaction and some will utilize a token method (a form of anonymizing) so that they only store a representation of the credit card. Then there are others that are still either lazy or ignorant of the importance of protecting this data.

I recently had a personal experience where a company asked me to send them my credit card information in an email. I refused to do that but agreed to a phone transaction. This is not a completely secure method either but my assumption was that the person on the phone would be keying it into a secure transaction system. That was not the case. Two weeks later, my credit card had still not been charged and I found myself contacting the CISO of that company. Yes, the company was big enough to have a CISO and still handled data in this way. There are PCI regulations that require the protection of credit card data and yet insecure practices exist. For all I know my information is on a piece of paper on someone's desk or in their email system. I won't go into what company it was or why I even agreed to this but suffice it to say, I was not buying a pair of shoes; it was something I really needed to do. I also needed to cancel my credit card after that nightmare. One point in this is that laws and regulations will eventually have an impact, but companies that are only doing the minimum to comply with laws and do not have other motivation for managing their data will likely never be doing the best thing for themselves or for persons whose information they have.

Moving on from the credit card example, here are some principles expressed within GDPR:

1. Transparency to the person.
2. Use the data only for the purpose expressed at the time of capture.
3. Only capture data that is needed.
4. Keep the data secure and protect its integrity and confidentiality.
5. Don't keep the data longer than needed.
6. Be able to demonstrate compliance.

Bullets 3, 4, and 5 should sound familiar from general logical data management principles. We will look more in depth at specific methods of managing data throughout this book.

We have talked about some requirements that might be unique to PI and PII data. One of the critical preparation aspects of handling and managing this data and the ability to be prepared for "anything" is additional metadata. We have previously talked about the required baseline metadata for all data and this adds more specifics to the attribution. Just because you have something called name as a label, does not mean that it is PII data or even a name at all. Likewise, if the label is not "name", it does not mean that it is not actually a name of a person. Labels should not be relied upon for definition of the data for any data. Adding attribution for type, category, or classification of data may be very helpful in the preparation for the unknown, but caution should be used to not tightly couple to a detailed element level metadata. Doing so would make it very difficult to maintain as the scope of types, categories, and classifications will change over time. In most cases, good element level metadata can be *mapped* to those higher-level categories *outside* of the metadata.

There is one aspect specific to PII that I do want to touch on here before we move on. The questions have been asked regarding whether or not you need the data or know what you will use it for, but let's take it to the next question. Where and for what do you need to know the identity of the person? Again, anonymization could come into play or just simple filtering.

As discussed in the section about laws, the definition of legal is continually moving. If your plan is to react and manage to every new definition, you will never catch up.

If you look at the management of PI data which includes the three questions, the respect of the data, and the usage of the data, it looks very much like the logical data management of all data with a few very specific principles added.

Summary of Privacy

Why so much time on privacy? It is not because it is the single driver for data management. It is not even because it is the most important one. It happens to be one that company leadership probably understands more than others because of the associated laws and potential penalties. As the laws and their enforcement increase, so will the visibility. It is very important to not take this *single* approach, but rather use it as a motivator to understand the holistic benefits of managing data.

Many companies will put resources and focus on data privacy with just the limited scope of data privacy. They are and will be chasing shadows. Logically managing data is the best approach to prepare for whatever comes in the future related to privacy laws.

Let's look at the summary of the points related to managing the data rather than assessing history and projecting the future. The key indicators for managing data from this chapter are:

1. Make sure that the definition of PI data is understood as being any data that is or *can be* associated with an identified person.

2. Make sure that your metadata for anything that is PI includes the method used to capture the data. This can be an essential component of compliance.

3. Understand the usage of the data.

4. Consider limiting exposure through reduction of data, i.e., not collecting or keeping data longer than is required, anonymizing where possible, limiting access, and limiting duplication / proliferation.

5. Answers to the three questions are still critical as a basis for PI data.

Chapter 5

DATA GOVERNANCE

All I can say to begin this chapter is Wow! Data Governance is an elusive beast for many and its definition and scope seem to be a moving target. Data governance and data management are sometimes used synonymously and others might say or act as though they are mutually exclusive. I believe it is neither. There is a relationship between the two and I don't know that the world will ever agree on the specific details of the definitions of both; many have tried and there are some good resources to utilize in the pursuit of your definitions. One that I consider to be on the top of the list is DAMA International.

The DAMA Guide to the Data Management Body of Knowledge (DAMA-DMBOK) has a well-known diagram of the Data Management Framework (aka the "DAMA Wheel"). The updated second edition of the DMBOK wheel defines 11 Data Management Knowledge Areas[1]. These might also be referred to as functions or disciplines of data management and one of the eleven sits right in the middle with the other ten surrounding it. The one in the middle is *Data Governance.*

The other ten functions, in no particular order, are data architecture, data security, metadata management, data warehousing and business intelligence, data quality, reference and master data, data modeling and design, document and content management, data storage and operations, and data integration and interoperability.

Relationship to the three questions

If you look at all of the functions on the wheel, including data governance, the three questions touch all of them. For many, it not only touches them but completes them as well. What concepts can be added to the three questions to make the underlying purpose and core principles complete for all data management functions? I believe only two are needed and we have already addressed both of them in some way. First, we have talked about treating data with respect from the beginning of the book; this will incorporate all aspects of the security and integrity of the data. Second, we talked about the usage in the chapter on privacy; usage addresses the usability and availability of the data. You can have the highest quality data and the highest security, but if it is not usable it arguably has no value to the business and has been a waste of time.

The combination of the three questions and two concepts looks like this:

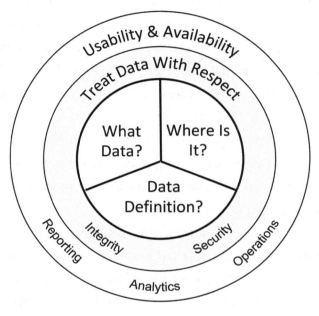

Figure 5-1

The three questions are at the center of circle. Everything *should* start there. Working outward from the center, how do you know the requirements for security or the measurements of integrity without knowing what and where the data is? And outward from there, you can hardly claim that you had realistically and accurately used the data without knowing what it means, the location of the authoritative source, and that the integrity had been preserved. If the answers to the three questions and respect are not in place prior to the usage of the data, it is too late. This is a pretty straightforward sequence with fairly obvious dependencies and yet time and time again I see people and companies just going right to the outer circle (the last step) and using the data. As has been stated, some knowingly skip steps and others "assume" that everything before the usage has taken place.

What is Data Governance?

Wouldn't it be nice to give a real short answer to that question? I can't, at least not yet. It has been referenced that data governance, from a DAMA perspective, sits in the center of all of the data management functions. What does this mean to sit in the middle? You can draw obvious conclusions and I am not going to quote DAMA here, but I encourage you to look into and learn from the resources available from and through DAMA [1]. If your definition of data governance is not about managing data or your scope is outside of the management of data, you are going down the wrong path. This is not to say that there should not be initiatives and committees formed on how to use data in new ways but that is not data governance.

The list of data management functions surrounding data governance is, in itself, an explanation of why there is so much debate and disagreement over the ownership of data governance. If you look at the roles and organizational placement of those roles pertaining to each of the functions, you will likely find them spread across the organization with many of them being in IT. Doesn't it make sense that if the majority of the roles lie in IT that the ownership and control of the data governance goes with IT? No. If you look at the general relationship between business and IT (and some may disagree with this), the business drives the intent, need, and definition of the business and IT assists in making it happen. If IT fills most of the roles, putting it at the center of data management brings to mind the concept of the fox watching the hen house.

There are a couple more aspects of this debate and one is the three questions. If all capabilities are dependent upon the three questions, it is important to understand who has the answers to the three questions. Knowing *what* data is needed by the business is certainly a business aspect. Knowing what data needs to *mean* and for what purpose is certainly the business. Where the data is can be the business but now we get to the realities. Knowing *where* are all of the places that the data can be is probably better suited to IT. Knowing what the data really means based on its technical implementation has IT involvement, hence the debate.

I referenced the need for a top role earlier in the chapter on data strategy. This is another spot where the importance of that role is very evident. Regardless of where you find the definitions of govern, it will likely contain the words and concepts of *authority* and *control*. These functions are essential to any governing body including data governance. These two words are also the reason that attempts at data governance fail. A data governance initiative without them is not governance by definition and many initiatives have neither of them. One of the primary reasons they do not exist in data governance initiatives is that they are trigger words. Data users, which are most everyone, react to those words as though they are oppressive and will prevent them from doing their job or at least make it harder. Without the knowledge or ability to make governance an enabler rather than an oppressor, leadership will typically buckle to the demands of the data users based on their misinformed perceptions.

Another reason that authority and control may be lacking in data governance is the belief that authority and control are unnecessary. If leadership takes the position that they are not necessary, then they should be brave enough to say that data governance is not necessary and stop pretending or putting up a facade. Company leadership knows that data governance is something that they *should* be doing but that is where it breaks in many companies. I hope this book will help change that.

So far, we have covered that data governance is central to data management, crosses business and IT, and needs authority and control, but authority and control of what?

Scope and Priorities of Data Governance

Govern with the authority and control of what? The scope, in this context, is about which functions or aspects of data need to be the focus for data governance. If you consider all of the disciplines that fall under data management, some of them are likely far better managed and addressed than others in your organization. Keep in mind that I am referring to company-wide management. With that in mind, the disciplines most in need are likely prime candidates for focus. It is also very likely that the ones that are in a position to answer the three questions are the ones that are less mature and need more focus.

Before defining the scope and priorities, an assessment of data management disciplines is in order. This is not necessarily an assessment of the effectiveness of data management in the disciplines, rather just start with the existence of the discipline. It is highly likely that an organization of any size has some structure and roles around functions such as security, database management, and a few others. As stated, these are not the areas that are most likely to be able to answer the three questions; they are generally more technical design and implementation areas. This also aligns with the approach to a data strategy in understanding what you have and plugging into the existing people and processes that work.

Understanding the capabilities that exist and whether they apply to the three questions does not mean that they do not have involvement in data governance, quite the contrary. All of the disciplines have some level of relationship and even interdependencies, so involvement across all disciplines is essential in the data governance initiative.

Keep in mind the focus on answering the three questions. Just how do the three questions relate to the scope of data governance? You cannot do anything effective with data without the answers to the three questions, so they are the beginning. Therefore, we start at the beginning to govern because it is the most impactful.

What - Let's break it down even further and start with *what* data you have; one of the "easiest" questions to answer. That does not mean it is easy but consider starting with the types of data that you have. What are the data domains in your organization? It may be that your industry already has standard data domains defined for the purpose of data warehousing or purely for ease of discussion. Defining the initial domains is the place to start defining the *what*, as well as being a key initial scope of data governance. You can't govern something that you have no means to discuss. A few examples of domains could be customers, products, sales, inventory, and contracts. Keep in mind that these examples could be either too high-level or too granular for your business model and business size. Also keep in mind that there we will a number of levels below the domain level to further define and group data. We will get into that design in a bit; right now, the purpose is to try to gather the "type" of data that you have in order to begin the work that falls below it.

I am going to take a shot at listing a number of key steps to defining the data domains in a somewhat sequential order, but keep in mind that the sequence will depend on your organization's current state and culture. That being said, following the logical approach, some steps must occur before others or you will waste your time:

1. It should be clear by now that leadership support and structure is essential. This applies to even defining domains or you will not have the appropriate participation.

2. Determine your *initial* key participants (roles). These are likely existing roles in related data management disciplines as well as the roles that sit "above" the domain level (more on these roles in the next section). You can't fill the domain level roles until you have identified the domains.

3. Define data domains – How to define domains should be somewhere: Each industry probably has a starting point

either through their related business organizations, data warehouse industry specific models, or the internal resources available.

4.   Identify domain leads and verify domain definitions.

5.   Find/define the next level of "data sets" under the domains – This is where the real work begins at this level and the next two levels down. The actual data elements are usually about three levels down from the domain. This is where a significant amount of the ongoing governance time will be spent. The structure of the hierarchy of managing data will be covered in detail in the chapter(s) on methodology.

Meaning – This is the definition of the data and the associated metadata. As mentioned previously, metadata can be stored and managed at different levels. Every level of the data, from domain on down, needs definition. People will usually think element level metadata, but it starts with the domains. The meaning of the data will be found to be a surprising endeavor. The appropriate people involved in the collection, definition of need, and the usage of the data typically exposes discrepancies between what it was thought to be, how it is used, and what it really is. The two lowest levels of this will certainly produce the most inconsistencies and discussion. The domain definitions may seem like a challenge because they are so high-level and contain so many sets of data, but the domain has the benefit of being defined solely based on what it should be. The lower levels force reconciliation between the discrepancies and in some cases will create the need for operational changes in order to resolve.

Where – Where, in its entirety, is probably the hardest of the three questions. This is why it is a strong recommendation for data governance to apply a master data method. Understanding the one authoritative source and governing to it is extremely important and certainly an in-scope item for data governance. That does not mean that all of the "other" locations of the data are not important, but those locations are better off being operationally managed by other data management capabilities based on standards and guidance from the Data Governance Office and the CDO.

We have talked about metadata and the different levels that it can be assigned. We have also introduced the terms of data domains and data elements. This is a rudimentary diagram of the hierarchy of the data discussed and the various levels that can hold definitions and metadata.

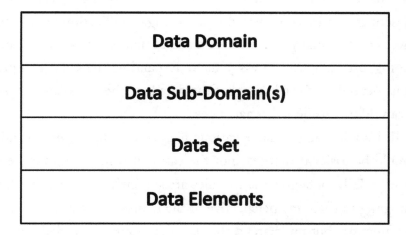

Figure 5-2

The labels on these levels are not that important at this point and they may be known by other names. The concept is the important aspect at this point. These levels will be discussed in much more detail in the chapter on methodology.

Roles within Data Governance

There are many roles related to data governance. It is a reality, in many companies, that data governance is an add-on ask to a person's "real" role. Which one suffers under pressure? As with the top role (CDO), it is important that some key roles do not have conflicts of interest or time in their execution. I also understand that there is a cost to this and even though I believe it is extremely important to the company and will pay for itself, it may be something that is eased into.

It is also possible that you have people in roles that could also represent a data governance role, such as a data steward. Utilizing existing roles and resources can be a good idea, but I would add at least one caution to this. It is often that this person represents an application, report, system, or department. As previously stated, an application or department cannot "own" data; data is owned by the company and must represent the entire company, not just a single application or viewpoint. I have seen this many times where a silo of data distorts the company's meaning, use, and even access to data. Expanding the scope of a person that is focused on the silo to what the data is to the company is possible but can offer considerable challenges.

Roles are going to have various names in different organizations. It would be easier if that was not the case but some data management and, especially, data governance roles are somewhat of a moving target. I am going to share my perspective of the names of the roles along with their function, but understand that the functions are needed regardless of the label you put on the role. The only requirement for the role name is that your organization understands what it means. I actually do not like saying that, but it is better than getting caught up in debates over names and getting little done.

Here are some of the key roles:

- **Data Governance Executive Board Members**: The highest level in the organization that supports the initiative and provides authority for it to work. Ideally, the CDO that reports to the CEO or company Board of Directors is the chair of this board. The board members should be the executive representatives of the participating organizations. This will vary greatly across companies, but should be expected to include both IT and business executive level representation. Most of the operations, as with any board of directors, is not done at this level.

- **Data Governance Lead**: This person is the operations and facilitation lead of the data governance initiative. This person would likely have direct reporting staff in the Data Governance Office that manages the day-to-day operations, communications, standards, reporting, and roadmaps for the work to be done.

- **Data Governance Office**: The roles and the number of people can vary from company to company. In most companies, the data governance lead cannot manage the operations and administration of all of the various operational domain level activities. Standardization across the various groups is essential in being able to bring meaning and usability to the company's data. This is the group that does that. In addition to administration and standards, another very important function of the DGO is education; education of the masses.

- **Data Steward**: This is typically a domain-level role. The person that is the point on the monitoring, assessment, and general day-to-day oversight of a particular data domain. This person understands what quality and integrity of the data means for that domain. It can be argued in theory that everybody has a data steward role. This is not the theoretical feel good role of being a good company citizen; it is real operational responsibility and accountability. This role, as with other roles in data governance, should not have alternate priorities or conflicts.

- **Data Custodian:** A data custodian is very often based in a technical role. It is even possible that the custodian has little knowledge of the data itself. The custodian is the protector of the data on a day-to-day basis and can speak to the nature of its integrity. Think of the custodian as the bodyguard. There is responsibility in this role of being able to attest to protection of the data and who has access and/or the ability to manipulate the data.

- **Domain Lead:** This role starts to get into the structure and operations of data governance. This person leads the group that governs data at the domain level. The group is made up of subject matter experts that have real operational knowledge of the details of the data within the domain. Subject matter experts will likely participate in the group on a very part-time basis and it is the responsibility of the domain lead to manage the meeting, agenda, and keep the group focused on their purpose.

- **Supporting Roles**: A number of these will come from the data capabilities in data management that surround data governance. Security is a good example. Security will likely have input in some cases regarding decisions that might be made and will be able to express the security ramifications. Another supporting role that is *not* a direct data management role might be legal. There are certainly potential legal ramifications to data decisions.

Some of these roles will show conflicts and alternate priorities faster than others. We have discussed that data is the focus and not an application and some roles may show that conflict very rapidly. Whether it is a business user of an application or IT development or support of an application, separating themselves from that application role can be extremely difficult. As long as someone reminds them of the potential conflict, they are extremely beneficial as real-world input.

The Groups of Data Governance

Regardless of the specific structure, it is important to have a structure. The structure, roles, and responsibilities enable the process that is required to make for consistent and functional data governance.

Here is the very high-level hierarchy of the groups involved:

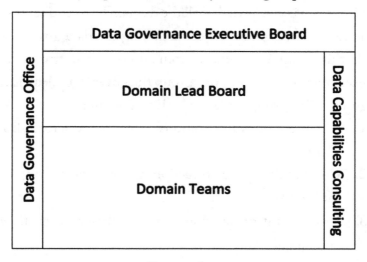

Figure 5-3

Let's start at the top. The **_Data Governance Executive Board's_** most important role is providing support and allocation of resources. The people that make up this group should be executive level so they are not likely going to feel good in a "support" role. This is a reason to make the group a leadership and directional group whose function is to support the effort, approve proposals and priorities, assign resources, and resolve roadblocks. With this group of leaders, it is again worth mentioning the importance that the chair of this board has a position, such as CDO, in the organization or the group is at risk of spinning. Most people in this group do not have any experience with data management or data governance and may want to make it something it is not in order to support their role in the company. This is one of the first groups that needs to understand the likely cultural shift that needs to take place and that the governance process is an enabler rather than a hindrance. It is very likely that people in the various roles within the data governance program are in a reporting structure outside of the data governance process to someone on the executive board.

The next level down from the executive board is the **Domain Lead Board**. This team is comprised of all the domain leads and representation from the Data Governance Office, including the data governance lead. People in this group likely report, from an HR perspective, to someone on the executive board, but in this group the governance lead is the chair of the group. This group serves a few key functions:

1. It is the point of operational consistency across all Domain Teams.

2. Communication of direction and standards happen within this group.

3. It is a point of discussion and escalation when topics cross domains.

4. Sharing discussion of what is working and what is not with other teams.

5. This is where resolution can happen for determination of which domain is responsible for a data set or data element. Any data set or data element can only be managed by one domain.

The **Domain Teams** are where the majority of the team level work happens. This team takes operating direction from the domain lead and the DGO. This team is chaired by the domain lead and consists of the subject matter experts from across various operational groups using and managing the data in each domain. The size of this team can vary depending on the diversity and size of both the organization and the domain. It would be difficult to imagine a team smaller than 4, and a team bigger than 10 is probably unmanageable. This count does not include the additional consulting representatives or the special guests. The count of 4-10 applies to the "voting members" who are expected in all discussions. This team has a few key functions:

1. They approve the single authoritative location for data within their domain.
2. They approve all definitions and metadata related to any level within the domain.
3. They approve the creation of new data elements within their domain in order to help avoid redundancy and conflicts in data.
4. They review status of data steward reports and provide input.
5. They approve the new usage of data within their domain. This is likely limited to situations where the understanding of the meaning/usage of the data is questionable.

The **Data Governance Office (DGO)** sits on the side of all of the levels of governance hierarchy. The DGO provides guidance, standards, reporting, and support to all levels. This concept is one that allows for the Domain Teams to be working consistently in order to have output that works together across the enterprise. As details are uncovered, it becomes evident that sharing of information in a consistent way that can be automated is essential to streamlining an effective process and robust company-wide answers to the three questions.

Data Capabilities Consulting is not really a team that acts as a team in most cases, but they all have the same purpose to consult, support, and utilize output from any of the levels below the executive board. There is likely some membership on the executive board that represents these areas. Their first purpose is to help prevent the governance process from breaking standards that might have been implemented outside of the governance process. Legal and security are good examples of areas that might have specific regulations to adhere to. If the scope is well defined, this shouldn't happen, but I can almost guarantee that it will. It is to be expected however, that the supporting teams will benefit from understanding decisions made by the governance teams. It is very likely that they will be impacted in some way.

Process of Data Governance

We now have an outline of the structure of the people and teams involved with data governance. None of that is of any benefit without a process. The process should be covered in a data governance charter. Yes, a charter. This needs to be a formal initiative with accountability, responsibility, and purpose. The roles, scope, and purpose should also be in the charter. Some of your charter may dictate variations of the processes presented here but consider this a guideline to work from.

Meetings - By the very existence of "teams", there is a need to collaborate and much of that is via meetings. Outlining meetings does not prevent the use of technology collaboration tools when appropriate. The executive board should meet at least quarterly to begin with. The members certainly can vote to make them more frequent but they should not be less frequent until a very well-oiled machine is in place or the executive level may tend to become complacent in the effort. The agenda for these meetings should be status reports of progress, presentation of issues/requests that have been raised to the highest level for resolution, and topics submitted by any board member. In addition to the operational content of the meetings, a significant amount of time in the initial meetings could be spent on education. The DGO is responsible for setting up the executive board meetings, the pre-read agenda, and publication of minutes.

The Domain Lead Board should have at least monthly meetings initially. As with all recurring meetings, they can always be cancelled if there is nothing on the agenda. This is a place for discussing the progress toward initiatives, concerns about process, overlapping data, and dissemination of information from the executive board and the DGO. The DGO leads this meeting and, as with the executive board, is responsible for the publication of the agenda and recording of minutes from the meeting. It is important for other meetings to have *alternates* but the Domain Lead Board is probably the most impacted by having missing representation. If the domain lead cannot make the meeting, they should send an alternate that is trusted with the same voting rights.

The Domain Teams will likely need to meet at least weekly. Getting participation could be challenging because, for the SME members of this team, it is likely a "volunteer" position on top of their regular job. They are the daily users, creators, and managers of the data within the data domain. They will likely care about getting the data that they are dependent on in order; the challenge is more likely to be with their management. In respect of everybody's time, it is important to have a clear agenda and move the meeting along. End early if the topics are complete. The domain lead is responsible for organizing the meetings and moving the meeting along. It is also perfectly acceptable for the domain lead to delegate some responsibilities to an administrative role that could be filled by the data steward for that domain. This will depend on the organization structure and time and resources allowed. It is more important that the work gets done and that it is clear who is responsible in the charter. There is also the concept of this team setting up subgroups or a task force for special initiatives to complete or investigate and bring back to the group. This can be very effective and respectful of people's time or interest. These task groups can meet as frequently as they deem necessary or possible.

Existing processes - Existing processes should play an important role when they can be related to a function of data governance. It has been mentioned that doing an assessment of existing roles and processes is a good grounding exercise for a strategy. This can also be particularly helpful when addressing the authority and control aspect of governance. I suspect that there are existing approval processes in your company. They could include things like purchasing, changes in policies, budgets, code deployment, and IT change management processes.

Any place there is a related step can be an opportunity for "sharing" the approval process. Let's start with some obvious ones such as data changes, changes to databases, creation of new data, modification of data structure or names, or moving data. Whenever processes or people are involved in adding new data to a system, is there a checkpoint before production deployment? There likely is. Can the small additional requirement/check be made to ensure that they have defined the data before adding it to production? This simple validation can add significant impact to operationalizing data governance. It's not a new checkpoint, but rather checks to see that ridiculously simple requirements are met. Do you know what this data is and where it came from? Do you really want to say that is too much of a burden? Would you refuse to validate that it is not redundant to or in conflict with data that already exists if there was a team that could do that for you? When the objections to these simple checks that plug in to existing processes are brought to light, they should look pretty silly.

Obviously, this process is a catch-point at the development, so look for processes that are earlier in the timeline and interject education of data governance impacts and process at those points.

Escalations will certainly be needed so a process needs to be in place. Let's put escalations into two categories, the ones that dispute the governance decisions and the internal governance disagreements.

Disputes against the governance decisions are more likely to happen in the early stages. Understand that if there is not authority or consequences there will be no need for dispute because people will just do what they want, and you might as well stop pretending to have a governance process and call it data recommendations. Governance is likely a change and people will test the process just like children test their parents. You may hear things like, "They told me that I had to define the data and I don't have time" or "They said that the company already has that data so I need to use that rather than creating my own and that is not what I want to do because it will cost more". Depending on the leadership, these should be easy to resolve. Don't have time to define the data? Who is going to buy that? It will take far more time to complain about it. It will cost more? That is a real common statement made in many companies and very often it goes unchallenged. The viewpoint of the company, in this example, should be that it is very difficult to believe that managing two sets of data, that are supposed to be the same (that will not be), is cheaper than one authoritative instance. These types of complaints will give light very rapidly to the commitment of senior leadership to data governance.

Back to the actual process. A good place to start the escalation is to check with the member of the executive board that is closest to representing the person or group having an issue with the governance decision. It is not only appropriate to include them, but it is the fastest way to resolve the escalation. They are the one person that can say, "You need to do what was decided". This ends the escalation because if they are not willing to support the escalation, it will go nowhere. This single member of the executive board can end the escalation by declining it; they cannot approve it on their own. If the member of the board agrees with the escalation, the DGO is notified and if it cannot be resolved with them, they will convene the executive board. Some escalations may be urgent to resolve, so they may not wait for the standard process of the next executive board meeting. An alternate method of information sharing and voting should be in place. Whatever the decision, the DGO will record the decision.

Decision options should also be defined. There are three basic options: approved, denied, or exception. To be clear, approval of an escalation is an exception to governance standards and the reason needs to be documented. The exception does not apply to any future instances and does carry requirements to remediate. An exception has conditions. A condition could be to go to production but resolve the issue within x weeks, or to resolve at some point in the future when some identified trigger is reached. As stated, with a strong governance process these types of escalations should diminish with time.

Escalations for internal governance disagreements are a very different escalation process. If the disagreement is with the Domain Team, it is escalated to the DGO. The DGO can determine if the disagreement or inability to draw a conclusion is appropriate to be resolved by the DGO, bring to the Domain Lead Board, or go directly to the Data Governance Executive Board. If the decision can impact other domains, either because the data crosses domains, or it clarifies an operating process, it should go to the Domain Lead Board. If it cannot be resolved there, it would escalate to the executive board. If the Domain Lead Board resolves it, the escalation conclusions would be included in Data Governance Executive Board reports.

Issues requiring funding or resources – This one is going to vary a great deal but regardless of the process, it is very important to know what it is. Let me give you an example. The Domain Teams identify a challenge in meeting their workload and the lack of tooling or resources is the only thing holding them back. They escalate to the DGO and if the DGO has funding, it can end there. If the DGO does not have funding, it can go to the Data Governance Executive

Board. Depending on your organization's funding process and the Data Governance Charter, the executive board may not have funding approval but may "support" funding. Maybe it is the CDO that has the funding capability? I understand that there are budgets and planning is needed, but the point is that people need to understand the situation prior to entering into a request process that ends with "I'm sorry, I don't have the authority". Funding is part of the organization and data governance initiative. There clearly needs to be justification, but money and resources will be necessary and need to be committed. People will see progress and support and they will likewise see the lack of them.

Some of these processes may have seemed to go into too much detail. It is not a complete list of all of the processes and situations that should be considered. The process may vary with the company but these guidelines are here to provide examples and potential consequences of actions or lack of actions.

The input and output of the Domain Teams – It makes sense to put some focus on the Domain Teams since all of the details and "real" work happens at this level. Where does the agenda come from to have that much to discuss? Assuming that this is a new process and a formal review process for data has not been in place, there is the existing data to review. Reviewing existing data for the minimum answers to the three questions can take a long time so the new data and changes being initiated by projects cannot wait until that is done. This concept applies to many initiatives that attempt to implement new standards and processes to an enterprise. This has been equated to changing the tires on the bus while going down the road at 60 mph. You need to answer the three questions for the existing data, but you also need to ensure that the new or modified data is governed as well.

Having the baseline metadata complete for data that exists certainly helps in the effort going forward, but you cannot wait for that or you will be in a perpetual state of catching up.

This is actually a good sizing and frequency exercise for the Domain Teams. There needs to be enough time and resources to process the load of new data reviews and, in addition, process the backlog of existing data. After starting on the backlog, do a rough mapping of the time to completion. If it is twenty years, you may want to change something.

The existing data reviews come to the team via an internal team process. How does new work come to the Domain Team to review? Here are a few ways but be creative and as comprehensive as possible:

1. Leadership statement of the requirement to involve data governance in all new data, modification of data, new use of data, and new movement of data. Involvement with new data and modification of data should be required in all circumstances. The new use and movement will likely need some qualifiers depending on how those things work in your organization.

2. Plugging into existing checkpoint processes as discussed.

3. Team members knowing of work related to their domain.

4. An intake process is essential and needs to be more robust than, "call John". A consistent intake form across all domains will aid in the acceptance. The intake should also consider that the person or team submitting the form may or may not know which domain to contact. The DGO might be a facilitator of some of that request flow.

5. All intake requests need to be addressed in a timely fashion and tracked to completion.

The output can take various paths but consistency and reusability is key to all of them. A request for review will have results and the result types will obviously align with the type of request. It is important to record the results in such a way that they are reusable. In order to be reusable, the metadata of the request, as well as of the data, needs to be searchable. Who made the request, what type of request, the data involved, and results of the request are examples of necessary information. Where are you storing the answers to the three questions? Many of the requests and internal initiatives will be about answering those questions. Where is the metadata stored? It cannot just be stored in meeting minutes or in word-processing documents. How will the company benefit from that? If someone is adding new data, the governance process should ensure that at a minimum the label, the one authoritative source, the domain where the data belongs (and maybe the data set), the definition, and the context are all documented.

Not all intake requests to the Domain Teams will result in conclusions that answer the three questions. Some requests may be about usage, process, or a general request for guidance. These conclusions, while not directly updating metadata, also need to be searchable for future reference by other domain teams or other projects. How do you accomplish that? All domains must record the required information in the same way or the information will be rendered useless. This information is one of those measurable items that shows progress and can be used for tangible benefits.

Tools

This book is not about any specific tools but tools are required for some functionality. From a data governance perspective, there can be a number of potential tools, but let's first look at the type of tool that exposes the value of the answers to the three questions. I am hesitant to even put labels on them because tools will come and go and so will the names, but we need a way to talk about them for now.

Let's call this a ***data dictionary***. It is capable of holding all of the metadata for all of the authoritative source data elements in the enterprise. The data does not need to be centralized but the metadata does. Centralization of metadata is the only way to find where data is, what it means in the enterprise and if there are conflicts. You should not need to know where the data is in order to find it. There are certainly tools that can do this or you can build your own. You can even start with something low-tech while the initial data is being collected.

There are ***discovery tools*** that can aid in the inventory of data elements in many locations that basically walk the repositories. These can be helpful but they are not a silver bullet. There are many tools that will claim that they are but be very cautious. You still need to verify the information and the metadata, so any tooling needs to allow for that verification and be able to track it. These types of tools can be helpful in identifying new data in the enterprise once there is a baseline that can be used as another validation point.

Governance process tools may or may not be specific to governance, but rather process enablement that includes forms, tracking, and reporting. This functionality can be built low-tech as well to begin with, but depending on the size and speed of evolution you may outgrow it sooner than you think.

Data lineage is something that we will talk about in the integration chapter but it is relevant to data governance and the usage of data. This is another one to add caution to the selection. There are some very good tools to use as aides but if someone tells you they can automate all of the data lineage, do not believe them. The tool may be able to discover actual lineage data, infer lineage data based on location of data and application code, or not find it at all. Again, there is not a silver bullet. There is a direct relationship between lineage and integration and we discuss this in much more detail in the chapter on integration.

I have a couple comments about tools in general. All of these tools mentioned have something to do with process. Do not let any tool dictate your process. You define your need first and then find the tool. If the process can work, it can work without a tool to verify the process. Tools should help the process scale and become more efficient and cost effective. Tools in general, not just the ones mentioned here, can be antithetical to your data management objectives. Many tools like to offer the bright shiny objects that sell products to the people that don't understand. This is another area to address by data management standards and review. How many tools, even in the space of data management and data governance, add security risks to data? How many unnecessarily replicate data? These two "features" of implementation are common in many tools. Make sure the right people are doing the evaluation and making the decisions.

Summary Definition

So, do we have a short definition of data governance yet? Let's take a look at where we have gone in this chapter. We talked about:

1. The relationship between data governance and data management
2. Combining the three questions with respect and usability
3. Governance definitions containing authority and control
4. Roles, teams, and processes of data governance
5. Financial and resource commitment
6. Consistent and reusable output from the governance process

Governing is a process so let's start with that and add to it:

An organized process (4) committed (5) to overseeing (3) the management of data (1) to ensure its integrity (2) and enable its effective and consistent usage (2,6).

It looks like we covered bullet points 1-6 so here it is without the numbers:

An organized process committed to overseeing the management of data to ensure its integrity and enable its effective and consistent usage.

Chapter 6

MASTER DATA MANAGEMENT

This chapter is about the *where* of the three questions. It is, however, only about the master location of that data and not all of the other locations that have copies of the data. Master Data Management is a term that is very often associated with a tool. That is not the case in this book. While an MDM tool can provide some functionality that proves useful, it can be complex, expensive, and typically a narrow scope of data in the scheme of your company's data. Master Data Management in this book might better be referred to as Distributed Master Data Management as a concept.

One Authoritative Source Requirements

We have referred to the "one authoritative source" of data. That is really the crux of this reference to master data management. This also starts to get into a piece of the methodology presented in this book. It needs more explanation than just being the authoritative source.

We just wrapped up the chapter on data governance and in that chapter we talked about the concept that the *one* master source needs to be the focus when talking about new data, definitions, and context.

The word *one* is extremely important in this concept. There cannot be two or more. This means that the master needs to service all consumers and all patterns for consuming the data. The concept of a single source and serving all consumers will be repeated over and over. These two concepts are absolutely critical to preserving the integrity of the data and supporting the concept of master data.

These two concepts and rules may present challenges for some systems, so further clarification is required. These types of challenges are usually technical ones and not challenges of concept. Technology advancements will likely change the technical solutions going forward, so I want to express the requirements rather than the solution.

An important aspect of the one source is that it is viewed, managed, and "owned" as one source. The one source is literal but not technical. Someone should not take this to the extreme, for example, that the one source needs to be a single hard drive, or a single server. Technology implementation allows for scaling of a solution to include RAID drive and server clusters for example. I just use these as examples of physical solutions, but the important aspect is the concept of those implementations still being managed as a single solution.

Another implementation example would be a system that is determined to be the authoritative source for data but cannot handle the "load" of all of the usage and integration requirements demanded by being the source. There are technical "attachments" to the system that can enable that. One example would be a cache. If the data is in a different physical location, there can be validation points to help ensure that it is not just a "copy" of the authoritative source. Copies can be a dangerous concept that warrants its own set of rules.

Here are a few checks to validate the technical solution:

1. It is *impossible* for the different physical locations to contain different data or any variations of data.
2. The "owners" of the authoritative source in its initial physical implementation *approve* the implementation model and are willing to swear, in court if necessary, that it is the same data.
3. Approvers include data custodians, data stewards, and data governance that encompass IT and business.
4. The purpose of another infrastructure location is purely for scalability.
5. No updates are done directly to the new physical location – all data is managed in the initial authoritative physical location.
6. The physical scaling does not change any security model, including access control and encryption.

Regardless of whether you refer to this as a single "system", it needs to be managed as one.

This may seem like a lot of detail about a physical implementation, but it is important to cover the qualifiers around the definition of a single authoritative source. It must be an absolute. Consuming data from another source must be consumed with the risk that it is different data. I worked with a great colleague by the name of Mike Bisek that used to say, "Similar is spelled D-I-F-F-E-R-E-N-T". When referring to data, that is *very* important. That is enough on the different data for now, as we will cover that in detail in both the integration and methodology chapters.

We have talked about what a single location (master) is, but master of what? Master of data of course, but at what level does the data have a master location? The individual element level would be very burdensome without a method to reduce the volume. The domain level is likely way too big to have a single master, especially in large companies. There needs to be a way to designate the single source for the data, and to this point we have referred to it as a data set. The data set needs explanation because it is a key to master data management as well as many other functions related to data.

Data Sets and The Evolution of a Data Topic

We have used the term data set a number of times, but data set means different things to people in different data management roles. A data set, in this context, goes by many names. Some might call it a record, but that also has a specific meaning to some that would be wrong in this case. We really shouldn't use data set or record because of their other legitimate uses that do not align here. We could call it a document but that has some specific meanings as well.

Let's try going back to the reason that we need a term. We need a way to talk about a group of data so that it has some meaning and can be referenced. Metadata can be attached to it and when you say the name people will have some idea what you are talking about. It is the name of a grouping of multiple data elements. Where does that leave us?

When you walk into the middle of a conversation and ask what the group was talking about, their answer would be the *topic* of the conversation. It is how you get the context of the conversation. The topic is the label that gives the conversation a very brief label. The purpose of putting a label on the group of data elements is so that it gives that grouping some meaning and context as well as the other purposes just discussed. The word topic has no previous conflicting definitions and while topic is generally used in regard to a conversation or writing, adding the word data to the word topic adds clarity. We will use *data topic* going forward to discuss a group of data. The requirements around a data topic are defined in greater detail in the chapter on methodology. At this point the data topic is associated with a single master.

Master Data Source Selection

Is the master data source the location/system where the data was first created? Many times it is, however sometimes it is not the best location or even a possible location. When those cases exist, it should not be more than one step away from the point of creation. If the system that created the data also manages changes to the data, it is by far the most desirable for that to be the authoritative source.

The system of creation may not actually have the need or ability for any data other than short-term storage, in which case it should be the next step in line of the movement of the data. A good example of that might be a register in a store or a tablet used for gathering customer interaction information.

Is the master data always the initial raw data that was created? No. The raw data should likely exist as a data topic and have a master, but "refined" sets of data (topics with a different name) can be *created* down the line in another master. The rules still apply to a new topic for a single master and a single authority for the related metadata. This is NOT a copy of the data; it is intentionally a new topic with all of the expectations of integrity, governance, and management as the original raw topic.

Does all data need a master? Yes. Take the situation where the system of origin does not need the data and it is determined by the appropriate governing bodies that the data does not need to be retained. It is just short-term, processing data. That is fine but, with analytics the way they are today, it may be that a copy of that data went to someplace to be used for analytics or some form of "data science processing". If that is the only place that it went, then that analytics location *is* the master by default. Master locations being created by default is not where you want to be. Consider the situation where you got a subpoena for that data and you needed to produce the data. Where is the most authoritative location of the data? Regardless of the intent of the location, its purpose, or the quality of the data, it is what you have.

This situation is working the mastering backwards and some would justly argue that it is not master data management. That is true because it is almost inevitable that the data has not been managed as a master. It is still the one (and only) source for the data. So, now we are coming full circle to the need to respect data and the need for a company-wide view of data. If one segment of the company, for one single purpose, ends up being the only place where the data exists, they now represent the company, the integrity of that data, and they *are* the one authoritative source. They will likely say that they didn't sign up for that, and they didn't, so they have been doing whatever they want with the data for their own purposes. This situation is the beginning of the reasons why an analytic or BI (Business Intelligence) system such as a data warehouse or a "data lake" should not be master data and the one authoritative source for any data topic.

How is that possible? Those types of systems create output such as reports and analytic conclusions that are, for the most part, an end-point. There are exceptions, of course, where an analytic conclusion becomes a new set of data that was created by that process. In that case, it needs to be managed as master data in a different way, with a different purpose, and in a different location than the data sitting in the system for analytic purposes. This new analytic conclusion data set (topic) needs to meet all of the requirements for the one authoritative source and manage that data topic in the appropriate way. The real risk is thinking that you can combine multiple functions on the same data in the same place. It does not work.

Another challenge obstructing appropriate master data management is the "convenience" of so much data in one place. Convenience comes at a cost. There are other perspectives on convenience, but for now let's focus on the data master in this chapter. We have already touched on the risk of data movement, the risk of dual functionality, and the risk of backing into a default master source for data. What about the argument of convenience? This is another place where data management leadership is essential because the perceived and familiar ease of access will win every time without it. Everybody gets all they need, whenever they need it and from wherever it is easiest. The integrity of the data is out the window. These appealing perceptions of convenience need to be addressed in a different way. There is clearly a use for analytic systems and data warehouses, so how are they managed in order to still provide the company-level data management? The primary method and principle is to require those systems with that function to be an end-point and not a source (other than under approved exception). Nobody "copies" data from these types of systems. There should also be an understanding and expectation that the data in these systems will not match the actual master system and the defensibility of that data could be challenging.

Regarding the analytic and reporting systems, think about how many times there is a need to change something about the data to make it useful for the reporting and analytic purpose. How much additional data is filtered, altered, or created in the process? It is important that a report, for example, clearly identifies the meaning for that data that is on it but not to the level of the full metadata, governance, mastering, and management perspective. It would likely crumble under the controls and nobody wants that.

How did we get to talking so much about analytics and reporting in a master data management chapter? We did because it is one of the biggest impairments to the success of master data management. I cannot tell you how many times I have heard stories of assumptions of the meaning of data being lost, the processing logic becoming outdated with the business, and the pattern of copies of copies proliferating because of "easy access".

Obviously, easy access is important but the support for master data management does not have to be a roadblock to the ease of access. That however is how most see it. There are a number of ways to solve for this with the combination of technologies, repeatable patterns of usage, and a governance process. The approach does not eliminate the need and usage of the analytic environments; rather it identifies the specific usage of the data and declares that it is "similar" data that is accepted to be "good enough" for its purpose. *Good enough* data is not data to try to defend in court or to jeopardize your environment by propagating it to other systems or using it for operational purposes with incorrect assumptions.

In addition to setting process and purpose around the analytic environments, a combined technical and process solution needs to address the ease of access concern for the master data source. There are a number of ways to do that but with technology advancements, the solutions will change rapidly. We will talk about some patterns in the integration chapter.

Master Data Management Conclusion

Master data management is a process, concept, method, and mindset that supports the principles of data management and assures the integrity and availability of one or more data topics from a single source.

Master data management is not dependent on the moving of data to a master source or a specific tool with a label of master data management. There is nothing wrong with tools, but make sure they fit you rather than forcing you to fit them. The actual data is not something that you want to lock into a given technology that endangers your flexibility and portability across solutions going forward.

While there are examples where the one authoritative source for a data topic has not been managed as master data, it should not be the intent and direction. Anything less than managing as a master adds significant risk in many ways.

Master data has relationships to a few of the concepts that we have already discussed:

1. The management of the metadata is at the master instance of the topic.
2. Data governance manages the metadata, usage, and ratifies the master location.
3. The entire circle consisting of the three questions surrounded by respect and usage is initially based on the master data. Any location beyond that inherits from the master.

The focus is the master because everything stems from the master. How and how much you let it stray will be the discussion of a few upcoming chapters.

Chapter 7

PROTECTING DATA

I would guess that the first word that comes to mind is security. Security has a connotation of being a technical capability. Regardless of what you call it, it is important to have a broad perception of the meaning when we talk about *protecting* data. We have already put security in the "ring" of *respect* that surrounds the three questions. Respect is a good broad term of which protection is a part.

It has been stated that this is not a technical or technology book, so there is no attempt made for it to be a book on how to implement security. However, security is one of the disciplines of data management, so recognizing the requirements as it relates to the broader topic of data management is important. There are new threats and challenges every day and keeping up with them is a challenge of its own.

There are a number of categories of protecting and securing data. One of them we have talked about quite a bit because it is key to the value of data; that is integrity.

There are two primary aspects to protecting the integrity of the data:

1. Data cannot be modified, deleted, or added to in any way outside of the approved method to do so.
2. The controls and monitoring are in place to assure that only the people or applications that are authorized are able to make the adds, changes, or deletions.

The other primary category of protecting and securing data is access to the data. This is above and beyond the integrity of the data. It is more about who can see it, use it, or move it. This is certainly part of protecting data, but some of these initiatives require more than what a security team might typically handle. A process for protecting the data against unauthorized use is one aspect of data protection that can happen in many ways:

1. The access point can be physical, where the location and method of storage and encryption might have an impact.
2. It could be basic access controls and credentials for accessing the system or specific data.
3. It could be restricting the movement of the data, including to and from the end user.

The first two examples probably fall into a category that most would associate with a typical security team approach. Others may be involved but the requirements and validations would usually come from the security team. The third, if addressed at all, might come under some generic company policy that has little to no enforcement or even a way to measure compliance. I would suspect that even if there is a policy, it is given little thought after its creation.

End user data movement is one of the easiest ways for data to not only get out of control and lose the *where* of the three questions but lose the protection. It can even assist in losing all three questions. If it is that much of a risk, why is it not addressed? We are probably back to the beginning of the book and the lack of understanding of both the importance and risks associated with data. This type of protection and respect of data is likely to be a culture shift. Unauthorized use of data is theft; it is stealing and yet most companies would not see it that way unless it was on a massive scale or pertaining to company "secrets". People are more likely to be fired for stealing a stapler than stealing data. Does that mean that companies value a stapler more than data? In some cases, yes. In many cases, they just do not understand. Of course, the details matter and many (not all) unauthorized internal users of data have "good intentions". So if they "need" access to the data that they are using, they should be given access. It falls, again, in the category of ease of access and the *perception* related to that.

It is very common across many companies that this ease of access is a justification to throw access controls out the window. It is so much easier to let everybody have "everything". Ask the CEO and the Board to share their home address and credit card information with every employee and see how that goes. It probably starts with good intentions because *some* people need access to *some* data. The people that have access to the data likely have the ability to copy the data to a new location, whether that is another system or their own computer. The further it goes away from that initial set of access controls, the less likely there is to be any control or even visibility. Ease of access and freedom to share drives it away. Many times, it is about who you know that has the data. If you are friends, there is often not a second thought about being helpful and sharing the data.

This is then not only a data protection and security concern but a data integrity concern, and we are again back to where we started. As was stated, this is not a book, or even a chapter, on the technical solutions and designs of data security. It is pointing out what is hopefully an obvious relationship with other aspects of data management. Protecting data is a major portion of respecting data.

Chapter 8

INTEGRATION

Integration is another one of the major keys to overall data management. It is also one of the things that is not even recognized by many. After all, anybody can (and does) do integration. It is not that integration is hard; in fact it is very easy. Treating integration as a component of data management is a big leap for most.

What is it?

Let's start by grounding in what data integration is. In the context of data management, it is simply movement of data. The definition is no more complex than that and with that definition it encompasses a wide breadth of data and technologies. The definition doesn't care if the data is moved or copied (for those that make that distinction). It doesn't matter where the data goes, for how long, for what purpose, what technology is used, who did it, or any other aspect that further clarifies that data moved.

Someone may say, "But I am just loading some data in a spreadsheet." Don't care. "I am just looking at data on a screen." Don't care. "I am not doing the movement of data; the tool that we use requires it." Don't care. "Everybody does it." Don't care. All of these examples and so many more are all data integration.

We are going to spend a lot of time on integration because it is so easy, "everybody does it", and it is one of the single most threats to both the integrity of your data and the ability to answer the three questions.

The Starting Example Diagram

Let's start with the diagram of an example of a very small amount of data movement.

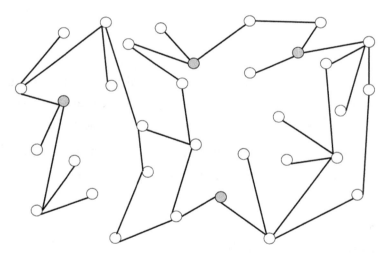

Figure 8-1

The dark filled circles are the master locations. The assumptions in this diagram are that:

1. The *one* master data location has been identified for a data topic.
2. There is only one topic per master location.
3. There is no modification to any of the topics during movement.

These are not realistic assumptions in a real situation, but we need to start with simple. We start with a simple example like this because I am confident that something like this, only *much* worse, exists in your company. In a medium to large size company, the number of master locations is more likely to be in the tens to hundreds. The number of data topics per system is far more than one, and the number of data movements is far more than the 6 or 7 shown per topic. Can you imagine what that diagram would look like? On a legal size paper, the ink would be solid black with no ability to follow anything. This is clearly not something that anybody would want to document and the thought of trying to pull it apart into something that would make sense could seem quite overwhelming. It would be hard to make the case that this is managing data.

By the simple assumptions that have been made, we can already tell that we have 4 data topics and that data is flowing from locations that are not the master. We have no idea what direction the data is flowing so let's add the direction and see if that helps.

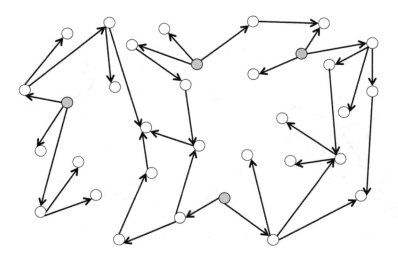

Figure 8-2

With the arrows we can now tell what direction the data is flowing. This is obviously a very basic and yet critical piece of information. Without the arrows we could not be certain of the source of each data flow. The master locations along with the direction of the flows allow us to know which locations are being used as a source. It also gives us the ability to walk the flow backwards. With the assumption of a single topic per master, we can also see the "daisy-chaining" of data. This is going from one to the next, to the next, to the next. This is the same as the concept of playing the game called "telephone", where one person whispers to the next and on down the line. What comes out at the end is very rarely what it started with even though that was the intent. This is a very common behavior in many companies and is a major obstruction to answering the three questions and to data management as a whole.

Take the diagram that now has arrows and apply a couple simple principles that we have already discussed multiple times. If you apply the principles that there is only one master per data topic and you always source from the master rather than from copies, it changes the diagram to look like this.

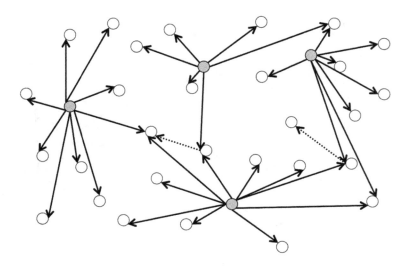

Figure 8-3

While this still has the same number of endpoints, it is much easier to see what is happening. It is not just about seeing what is happening, it is reducing actual complexity and risk. If all of the targets source from the same location, the probability of consistent data that still retains the meaning is far greater. This does not ensure complete consistency but eliminates a great number of hidden and unintended consequences.

You may notice that there are still two lines that are being sourced from a non-master location and they are indicated by a dotted line. Even with the assumptions, not enough information has been provided to determine the appropriate master source for the data on this line. We do not know what the data is. Both of these sources have received data from two master sources covering two different topics. Which topic is exiting the non-master, or maybe it is neither? The only way to know is to know what data the line represents on the diagram and that looks like this.

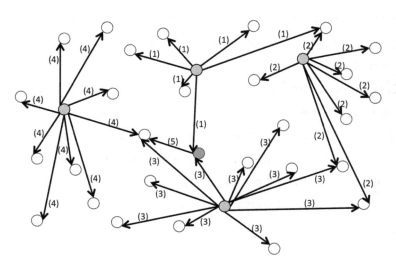

Figure 8-4

The two dotted lines in Figure 8-3 have been resolved and every line has a label indicating the data topic. Numbers are not descriptive data topic names but they are unique, so for now we know which ones are different and which ones are the same. The dotted line that was to the right was resolved by understanding that it was topic (3) and sourcing it from the master. The dotted line that was on the left was not as straightforward. The irregularity of the diagram provided a trigger to dig deeper and when we did, we found that it was neither topic (1) nor topic (3). It was actually a new topic with new data that was created from topic (1) and (3). This is not just the data topics combined; it is newly created data (5). If it was just a merge of the two topics, then the target would source from both masters to help ensure that the data was the same and to provide better traceability of the movement of data.

These are some very simple diagrams and there is obviously far more to integration than is represented in these diagrams. The purpose is to provide a basic concept of how integration can relate to data management and how consistent data flow diagrams can be a tool for data management. Diagrams are helpful from both a data governance perspective and an architecture perspective. Diagrams rapidly expose designs that break data standards or principles and allow them to be addressed.

It is processes and standards, such as this, that allow governance to scale without being a roadblock. From personal experience, I can tell you that with diagramming standards I can look at a diagram far more complex than these examples and tell you where the points of concern are (if any) in less than a minute. Without the standard, it would take multiple people multiple days to assess a solution, and that just does not scale.

Understanding the Complexity of an Integration Line

The line on a diagram looks simple enough but in most cases it is not. There are typically a number of steps involved in each line and each step is a potential point of failure. These steps are typically steps that are driven by the technical solution. The non-technical person should be aware that they exist, and technical people should be aware of their custodial responsibilities in design and implementing a solution. We talked about something similar in Data Capture so you should have the concept of multiple steps, but let's use an example that is specific to fairly straightforward integration.

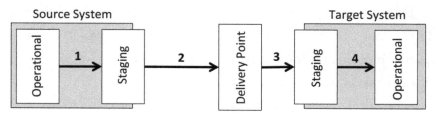

Figure 8-5

Not all integration solutions look like this. Some have less steps and some have more. This is not a "stretch" to make a point. It is an example that I would consider to be in the middle of complexity if people are willing to look at the details. This example shows 4 steps in the process, but it could be easily argued that it is eight steps because each step consists of a read and a write component. Each read and write component is a potential "point of failure".

Point of failure is a common term in IT and for some it may mean a physical failure. In this context, the reference to a point of failure is any point where there is handling of data that provides an opportunity for the data to be manipulated or lost. Before looking at each step, I want to outline a few potential failures that could be common to every one of the 4 steps depicted:

- Was the query to read the data written in such a way that will produce the complete expected results per the definition of the particular data topic?
- Was there any manipulation or filtering of data applied in the code that actually moves the data from the source of the step to the target of the step? If there was, it potentially changes the

topic to something else and will make it harder to document and maintain over time.

- Did the write to target complete for all data presented? If the process did not complete for every byte, is there a recovery process to ensure the completion?

These are pretty standard considerations in building an integration solution, but it is more than most would think of, which makes it a concern since integration has been made so "easy".

Let's take a brief look at each step:

1. The staging of data often occurs internal to the source system but regardless of where it is, it is at least two points of failure. It is "at least" because staging may execute with various triggers or at various frequencies and the triggers themselves may fail. This staging step is more likely to take place when the source system has some sort of operational use (which is most) in order to minimize impact to the operational usage.

2. Move to a delivery point. This is more likely to be the case when the data is pushed rather than pulled. This step has the same common potential failure points.

3. Move to target staging. This happens in a significant amount of integration solutions with good reason. It is another step that is not recognized by people that are not actually designing or building the solution. This is actually beneficial in helping to ensure that the data has the ability to make it completely to the target system. Ideally, the staging area has no constraints and has the ability to notify the integration technology of a failure, to enable a "retry". This also has the same common potential failure points.

4. Write to the operational target data store. This completes the integration line. It is a very common place to find logic that manipulates the data, especially in this type of integration

pattern. This is an endpoint and as long as it stays an endpoint, there is nothing wrong with the manipulation under certain parameters.

Each one of these steps, as we have pointed out, is a potential manipulation and failure point. One purpose of this dive into some integration steps is to understand that data can fail which causes additional risk to the integrity of data from any source other than the master. Other than the risk of movement and non-master sourcing of data, this starts the discussion of being able to understand where *all* data resides. It has been stated that the beginning point and focus of data governance is the master data, which is still true. However, we have also discussed that there is reason, not least of which is laws, to know where all the data resides. It is reasonable to expect that more than 70% of the data in your company is copies of data. Some may be as high as 90%. Copies of data are created via integration.

Integration Metadata – Data Lineage

Creating copies of data gets to the initial concept of data lineage. Data lineage will not only tell you where the data came from and where it went, it will tell you how it is different than where it came from. Doing this in project documentation may happen in some companies, but you will never find it again when you need it. Data lineage is actually the metadata about the data movement.

A comment was made earlier about tools claiming to automate data lineage. A comment was also made about the definition of integration. For the purpose of data lineage, we are not going to include integration to a screen. An application needs to integrate with data, so it is integration, but we are going to focus on the creation of "copies" rather than the fact that the data moved across a wired or wireless connection.

This type of movement is a concern for security, but we will not consider it in scope for data lineage and alternate locations of data.

It is good to have the container referred to as a topic to talk about data lineage. It aids in reducing complexity and increasing organization, but the lineage details inevitably will need to go the element level. It will be obvious when you understand the minimum metadata required for lineage.

At the topic level we need:

- Source system
- Target system
- Topic name

The rest is at the element level:

- Element label in source system
- Element label in target system
- Element location in source system
- Element location in target system
- Element transformations/modifications
- Element level failures of execution (such as the target location no longer exists)

There are a number of optional elements that could be included but this is the minimum. All of this information is stored as accessible configuration data in some integration tools. The existence of these elements in an accessible manner enables the tools that "discover" data lineage to actually work. It is important that this is not just documentation that can become outdated; it must be the actual execution configuration data. This is a good reason for using tools that enable this capability, but it is highly unlikely that you will hold all integration to tools that expose the required elements. It is more likely that it is a small percentage of your integration.

There are a few other general techniques that lineage discovery tools will enlist. Some will look at documentation such as java docs, but we all know that documentation is very susceptible to being out of date. Some will claim to be able to read all types of programming code. I have never seen this to be reliable. The complexity of various languages and coding styles makes it very unreliable. The use of variables alone can make it difficult at best. The code also does not account for any failures of execution. The third and most inconsistent and unreliable is comparing labels and data across multiple locations and inferring the targets and sources. When you consider even the simple first diagram in this chapter, the inference has no ability for logical and accurate conclusions. At best, it can provide a list of data that *might* be related for you to look at.

Assuming that not all of your integrations are implemented with tools that have extractable lineage metadata, you are realistically going to need to prioritize. We have already indicated that the master locations should be a priority but lineage is beyond the master. Considerations for prioritization include, of course, laws that require you to know where data is and potentially remove it. This is primarily the privacy-type regulations. There can also be data that you may be contractually obligated to remove on a specific timeline or on request. You may or may not have contractually controlled data. Obviously, the laws that impact copies of data are going to be high on the priority list and there are a few ways to address that.

Another priority is going to be data that is both frequently accessed and critical to the operations of the company. If you combine that with a scenario where the consumption of that data is heavily from a non-master, getting the lineage to and from the non-master source is going to be very important.

Even with bubbling the data in these categories to the top of priorities, it still results in a significant amount of work. Additional prioritization or layering will likely be required as well as alternate approaches to minimize risk. The layering approach is likely going to be the most realistic to speed up some answers. It does however have some dependencies. The first layer is what topics go from what system to what system. This is similar to our example diagrams that are just lines between systems with the name of a topic. This obviously assumes that you have topics named. If you don't, you may need to name them on the fly and resolve the overlap later. This is clearly not the best solution because it will create rework but it does give you a cursory view of where data is going. This is also assuming that your first priority is going to be topics that include privacy data.

At this point, it may be easier to see one of the potential advantages to anonymizing PII data. Any copy of data that has fully anonymized PII data takes the PII and the PI data out of scope for regulations and the priority of those flows can be reduced (not eliminated).

Clearly if you have topics and masters identified, you have a basis from which to work. The work is still challenging but significantly less. Don't wait for this reason to start.

Patterns

How many patterns of integration can there be? There are books about just integration patterns that are over 700 pages. We are going to cover the conceptual patterns that are needed from a data management perspective in a few pages. We will add some variations that are important, but we are going to start with just two basic conceptual patterns.

The first is point-to-point and it is probably the most common integration pattern used as well as the one with the most risk and inconsistency. The second is a hub and spoke or pub-sub (publish and subscribe) pattern. This pattern does not have to be a true pub-sub solution but is similar enough to be conceptually in the same category. We will look at each one separately.

Here is a simple point-to-point solution with four targets of the same topic:

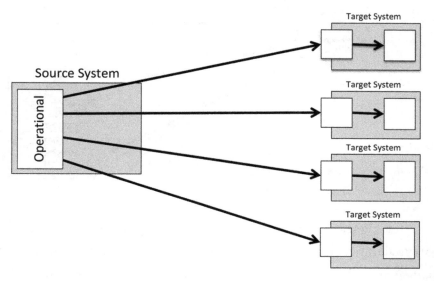

Figure 8-6

The point-to-point solution has no concept of any consumers of the data other than the *one* at the end of this solution. These are four independent solutions. All of the steps that we stepped through are built exclusively for each solution. In this pattern, the second step (delivery location) likely does not exist. Even if you add a staging area on the source as in the diagram that follows, the query to get the data from the source, the code to move the data, write the data to staging and to the target operational store is all unique to each integration.

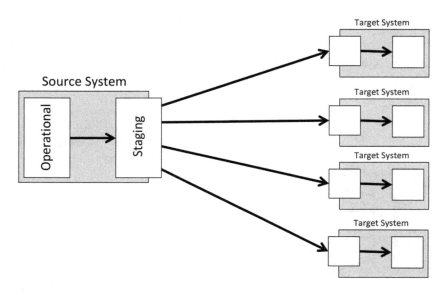

Figure 8-7

The biggest advantage to adding staging is that it lessens the potential impact on the operational source, which is not specifically data management, but does respect the operational nature of the data and the application at the source. Staging also has the opportunity to limit the amount of data available to be queried.

It is probable that a point-to-point pattern has the fewest number of steps, which you might think to be the most cost effective and most reliable due to fewer points of failure. Neither of these is true unless you restrict the consumers of the topic from the master to one single consumer.

There are negative impacts of multiple point-to-point solutions of the same topic starting from the very first step. Each consumer has their own query to get the data from the source. This means that inevitably they will be different. Even if the source system stages the data, the query against the data is specific to the consumer. If you share the query code execution to get the data, it is not point-to-point. If you copy the query and start out the same, they will never stay that way over time. Also, if something changes in the source system that requires the query to change, every query needs to be changed and tested rather than just one. With just the first query step, you have a high probability of systems getting different data and the cost to maintain is increased.

The rest of the steps in the point-to-point likely stay the same as any other integration pattern and likely have no further negative or positive impact on the cost or reliability.

The hub and spoke or pub-sub concept needs a little explanation because it actually encompasses a number of patterns but has some commonality across them. The first, and probably the most important aspect of this pattern, is that there is a common extract from the source system. This way, all consumers are guaranteed to at least start with the same data. This obviously does not guarantee that the data will remain the same all the way through to each target, but the modification will be deliberate rather than an unintentional difference in extract. In drawing the data flow diagram, the "split" in the flow to multiple consumers can happen at a couple of different places along the flow.

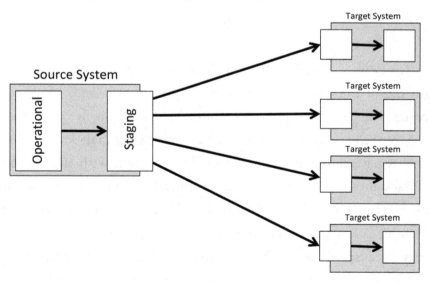

Figure 8-8

Wait a minute; this looks just like one of the point-to-point diagrams. It is. This is a data flow diagram and in this case the flow is the same. The difference, that you cannot tell from the diagram, is that the lines out of staging are being controlled by the single source vs. by each of the targets in the solution. This solution assures consistency getting to the target staging. A variant could be depicted as this:

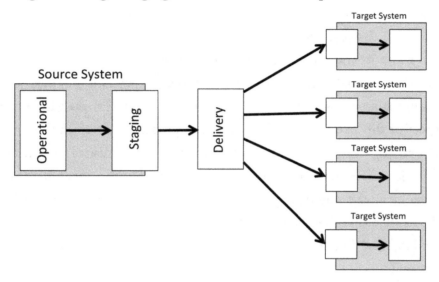

Figure 8-9

The flow could split where it is shown in this diagram or it could split right out of the source system as in the previous diagram. Regardless of where the data flow splits to various systems, it is likely that there are more steps in this type of pattern for a single target than a single point-to-point pattern but fewer over all. This diagram with the four lines coming out of the delivery area can technically be one line in execution with certain integration technologies. If the only integration of the data topic is a single system then point-to-point makes the most sense purely because of the number of steps and reduced risk and cost. The number of steps, reduced load on the source, reduced risk, and increased consistency is better with the hub and spoke concept.

Of course, hundreds of patterns are not going to fully fit in these two examples, but the considerations and concepts are usable across all patterns. Integration technology solutions will evolve but applying the objectives and requirements of data management to them will remain the same.

Reconciling Integration Design And Data Management Objectives

There are a number of perspectives when it comes to integration. We can start with the assumption that the reason to move the data is to make it more useful. After a number of decades in this business, I can assure you that sometimes moving the data is not required for the usefulness that is desired. It is rather, what is familiar and perceived to be the best or even the only way to achieve the objective.

From an integration perspective, cost is usually a significant driver to the solution. What is the cheapest and fastest? This is often assessed from the perspective of the single project at hand and may not consider maintenance or other users/projects.

Then we have the data management objectives, which you should be familiar with. We need the answers to the three questions, the respect of the data, and of course the usability and availability, which brings us to integration. Remember that the importance of the three questions and respect cannot be thrown out the window on the way to usability.

Being able to answer the three questions and the respect for data will drive a couple of principles *specific to integration*. The first might seem obvious when you say it, but in execution it is not.

Principle 1: Don't replicate data unless you need to. There is so much replication of data that could be done in another way or not done at all. There is the concept of "while I'm there I might as well take as much as I can because I *might* want it some day". This concept has been sold for many years in many companies and falls into the why not? It's not going to cost much more to move it and storage is cheap. Before you know it, you have hundreds or thousands of copies of data that you have no idea what or where it is. It easily gets lost because it wasn't needed and is not used. There are technologies that allow for the "look-up" of data as needed in operational situations. You should always ask the question, "is there another way?". The concept of "service-enabled" data has opened the doors to reduction of replication in many scenarios. I would say most operational scenarios are candidates for this model, making replication predominately justified for deep reporting and analytics.

Principle 2: Always source from the master. We have discussed this one enough that it is hopefully obviously critical to maintaining the integrity of the data.

Principle 3: Data replication happens by topic. As we have discussed, and you will see even more evidence of, there is no reasonable way to talk about data without having some sort of topic level name/ID. This does not mean that you need to replicate an entire topic, but in the hub and spoke pattern it would mean to push or make available the entire topic, and only the data that is needed is persisted. This allows for very manageable updates at the individual consumer level if needed.

Principle 4: Reduce the number of steps in an integration solution. Steps add risk to the integrity and security of the data. This includes the risk of failure and risk of manipulation. The step count needs to include a holistic data view that includes a single extract from the master for consistency where possible, the total steps across the topic for all integration points, and the number of steps impacted for maintenance/ change.

Integration is part of a data strategy. How it is done, when it is done, and the process surrounding it should all be part of the strategy. We have talked about integration impacting the three questions. In order to answer the *where* for all locations of the data beyond the master, lineage information is required. This brings us to the last integration principle for this section.

Principle 5: Produce auto-maintained lineage metadata. This is not always going to be possible but it should be the exception when it is not. There are a number of ways to attain this with either purchased integration tooling or custom coding. Process alone may help maintain the lineage data, but lineage metadata maintained outside of execution is likely to get out of sync.

Integration Tools

Everybody does it! You will find integration functionality built into most tools of any kind that you purchase. They may not call them integration, but phrases like "compatible with xyz applications" or "connectors" are very good indicators that they are doing data integration. That makes it easy, right? It very well may be making it a nightmare.

Let's try to separate some different types of integration tools into categories:

- Professional integration tools
- Custom coded solutions
- Integration embedded in other applications
- End user methods

Professional integration tools are tools that technical people are trained to use for the purpose of building and maintaining integration solutions. This is a broad category of tools and brands and there are some obvious big players in this category. Whether big or small, across the category they will cover every one of the hundreds of complex and simple integration patterns. This is the category that is most likely to provide accessible lineage metadata. Not all tools in this category will provide that, but you will be far less likely to find them in other categories. This is also the category that is most likely to enable the hub and spoke integration concept with pushing data to the availability of multiple targets. Since it is a smaller group of people that are trained in the use of the tools, it is also the category that can most easily have standards and governance in place.

The smaller group and the standards that can be put in place is also the reason that it can be *perceived* to be a slow, bureaucratic, and a costly solution. Another argument against this type of centralized integration is that it will likely involve "another team". Every project and every team probably prefers to do everything themselves because involving someone else "slows them down" and they can do it "cheaper" themselves. I cannot tell you how many times that I, and others in similar roles, have heard that. Allowing these arguments alone to win is simply abandoning data management. This statement does not mean that everything must be centralized, that projects cannot build their own solutions, or that there are not issues to be resolved with these professional solutions. This is not an easy road and is an example of why it was stated that integration must be part of a data management strategy.

There are certainly poorly managed "integration shops" that will delay, increase cost, and complicate integration for projects. The answer is not to let everybody do whatever they want with no traceability; the answer is to fix the process. The problems in this situation are almost always process rather than technology. In addition to simply improving the process, a high-level concept might be finding a hybrid solution that allows for a common team to build core reusable components and oversee or review the project or application team doing the detailed work. This still requires collaboration, which is often more a cultural or emotional hurdle rather than a technology or process one. Making a change in the use of the professional tools will require a willingness of all players to collaborate on a solution that meets the needs of both data management and ease of data availability. Visibility to process, monitoring, and status are important aspects of collaboration. This is actually a microcosm of the willingness and collaboration that is needed across all aspects of data management.

Custom coded solutions can be a legitimate solution. I have been part of custom coding solutions and participated as co-author of patent applications for some. I do believe in custom coding when it solves a problem for which there is no existing solution. Not everything has been solved and things can be improved, so custom coding is an option. Custom coding allows you to do anything, including enabling the lineage metadata for integrations.

There are two major sub-categories of custom coding. There are custom coded solutions that are built for the company as a reusable framework and those that are just coded for a single specific project or integration solution. It is the latter that is of the most concern. I would go as far as to say that it should not be allowed other than through some formal exception approval process.

Custom coding a single integration or project will bury the logic and the visibility of the solution. It will not only make it hard to find the answers to the three questions, but will also make maintenance of the solution very difficult. This is the equivalent of "hard coding" to a programmer, as though nothing will ever change – it will.

A custom built framework, when purchased solutions do not meet your needs, is an option that can work, but it should be developed with the same considerations that would go into product development. Evolution of the framework will likely need to happen and it should not destroy the existing use (backwards compatibility). Another advantage to this, as well as to the purchased tools that meet these requirements, is that when a global change needs to happen, such as a security enhancement, it can happen in one place with consistency rather than in many places. This alone is a very significant cost savings but also assures the consistency of implementation and protection of the data.

Integration embedded in purchased applications has become very common. It is used as a selling point for applications and in many cases it undermines the objectives of data management. Applications are sometimes built with what seems to be a mentality that they "own" the data that they *acquire* and hold from other sources. Applications that require the unnecessary replication of data, because it is easier for them, are not doing you any favors. I will not state as a fact that no tools in this category provide visibility to the lineage of the data, but I have never seen one. I have seen many that do not even provide the ability to interact with the data in any way within their application in order to know the answers to the three questions.

Allowing applications to implement the movement and management of your data outside of your data management policies and principles is handing your data risk, liabilities, and data integrity over to a company that has no more interest in your company than selling you a piece of software. I do not believe that is too harsh. Integration and data management is likely not their forte and they just see it as a simple piece of code that makes their work easier by managing the data internal to their system. They see it as a "selling point" and it works when people are not aware of the negative impact it has on data management. Some of these applications do not force you to use their integration solutions. If they allow you to use your own integration solution, please do so. If they don't allow it, beware. There are of course, as with anything, some exceptions where integration with a specific application might make sense when the applications are software partners and would be treated as a very tightly coupled solution.

Two major types of applications are operational systems and reporting/analytic systems. It should be remembered that regardless of the type of application, their purpose sits in the outer ring, beyond respect for data and the answers to the three questions. Operational systems are likely installed and managed by IT and "should" have appropriate controls and process for data management. While many operational applications may have direct access to the master data, we have eliminated that from the scope of this chapter because the data is not actually persisted in a new location.

Many of the reporting/analytics systems fall into the IT installed and supported applications. There are, however, the end user reporting systems that also include integration.

End User methods include some high-end solutions as well as ones as small as a spreadsheet that can connect to a data source. People might not typically think of a spreadsheet or other desktop installed applications as integration systems, but they absolutely are and appropriate management is in order. Some of it can be done via technical solutions such a limiting data movement or setting TTL (time to live) on the data. At a minimum, there should be policies and an approach defined for finding and removing data if needed.

Data consumption, outside of the integration aspect, is a topic big enough for a chapter of its own.

Integration Summary

The purpose of the integration chapter was not to turn this into an integration book even though this chapter was long enough that it may have seemed like it. From the beginning of the book, it has been pointed out that data leadership, as well as setting the expectation of cultural impacts, is required; this fully applies to integration. Conflicts presented between the current integration methods and a new data strategy can be resolved in a way that makes data more reliable, flexible, and cost effective as long as the data is given respect and the company, rather than the project, perspective is applied.

It is important for people in all data management roles to understand the potential impact of integration on data management. It is also important for those in integration roles to understand their responsibility and role in data management.

The first, and probably most obvious, impact is the number of copies of data. Not just copies of data but copies of copies of copies.... This has a tremendous impact on being able to answer the *where* of the three questions.

It is still true that focusing on the master is the most important initial focus for data management and data governance, but at some point all of the locations of data will have potentially significant impact. Security is one area where *all* locations matter from the start. The purpose of instantiating the principles of integration is to start setting the groundwork to prevent the situation from getting worse. The current copies can be slowly reigned in over time and via attrition. Lack of lineage documentation and daisy-chained data have been the root cause of data failures across many companies. A data strategy, governance process, and education of principles can all aide in that regard.

The question of where the data is located is not the only question impacted by integration. Many think that it is; however, the change that can happen to data is something to be very aware of, whether intentional or unintentional. Every step in an integration process is a point where not only failure can happen but manipulation as well. Everybody has good intentions, and they are doing what they think they need to do, but other users may not be aware of what has been done with the data. Assumptions will be made about the meaning and completeness of the data unless the appropriate principles and governance are in place.

I have seen and heard of hundreds if not thousands of inconsistencies of data across many companies. Companies may tend to shrug this off for various reasons. The reasons range from never assessing the data to not being willing to accept that their data is out of control. Some will think, "someone just made a mistake". Occasionally eyes open when people outside of the company point out the inconsistencies, such as business partners or the government. These are not one-off situations and people should take heed.

I want to make one more point about inconsistencies. Some people, in an attempt again to do the right thing and preserve the integrity of the data, will build yet another integration to compare the source data to the target. While this might be viewed as better than nothing, it is not a very robust solution and has many flaws. Data may not be in the same state due to timing or the data may be intentionally different so the comparison would require the lineage metadata. Some will use simple "record counts" but that does not ensure the integrity of the data and there are far better and more accurate ways to identify "dropped" data. Data should be managed and monitored for failures at each step.

Define your integration principles that support data management, build the governance process, and measure the effectiveness toward those principles. There are a number of types of governance processes that are possible. We have talked about data governance in this book, but depending on how your integration principles/standards are written, some of it may be able to be governed by architecture governance, which is more of a technical solution review that can support data management principles.

Repeating a few key points from this chapter:
- Replicate only when required
- Replicate only from the master
- Simplify the solution at the company level rather than project level
- Build solutions with automated lineage metadata

Chapter 9

REPORTING AND ANALYTICS

We eliminated the screen integration from the scope of the integration chapter and we are going to for this chapter as well. While this chapter may have some overlap with integration, its focus is more about the activities of the data after being moved or alternatives to moving the data.

I believe that we have talked enough about the operational usage of data, including the caution to not replicate unnecessary data, being careful of embedded application integration, and not sharing a copy of data. Operational systems are however very likely to create and be the master for new data, but they should not also become the source for data that they took from another system. This is a common *mistake* because of the "convenience" factor.

The Scope of Reporting and Analytics

That leaves the major type of consumption as being reporting and analytics. Reporting and analytics is a broad category that deserves a bit more granularity. Whether you call it executive reporting, metrics, analytics, business intelligence, machine learning, artificial intelligence, or any other new names that will come about, it is all in the general category of reporting and analytics. There are many ways to slice this type of usage. Some might tend to want to talk about terms such as data warehouse, cloud, and data lake when talking about reporting and analytics large volume storage. All of those are probably very large locations for data, but they are nothing more than storage until you apply one or more functions to them. The functions and the impact on data are what we care about, so let's try to stay out of the storage implementation method.

We can also assume that there are different levels/volumes of data ranging from the three large ones that were just mentioned, down to a spreadsheet on a laptop and everywhere in-between. Large size environments have additional considerations and potentially more functions but the smaller ones cannot be ignored.

Large Platform Considerations

We will look at some functions in the large environments, but first let's talk about some common considerations and behaviors with these platforms. The first consideration that we have already discussed is the mistake that is commonly made of putting multiple functions on the same data set in the same location. It causes problems in execution and it especially causes issues with the data itself. From the standpoint of these large reporting and analytics systems, it does not mean that you cannot perform multiple functions in one platform; it means that it cannot be on the same instance (internal location) of that data.

The next consideration includes having a management strategy, a governance process, and monitoring to ensure the appropriate execution. These large platforms rapidly become a company unto themselves from a data perspective. There is so much data that it can easily get lost and the answers to the three questions become nearly impossible to find.

I have heard many people talk about their data lake rapidly becoming a data swamp. This can happen in any large data platform. The *creation* of a new platform is the perfect time to get its management in order. Consider that people may be able to put data there without validation of accuracy, from non-master sources, and with no definitions. Then someone else modifies the data and duplicates it and then this easy access to lots of data becomes easy access to something that nobody should use. You have a swamp.

Speaking of easy access, the access controls put in place to see the data at the master should be no less on one of these platforms and yet often times they are. In addition to inheriting the security from the master, the definition and other metadata should follow as well. The meaning remains the same unless it is intentionally changed, which can be very likely in these platforms. Changing the data is okay but appropriate metadata is essential. With good management, these platforms can be a significant contributor to the integrity, clarity, effectiveness, and usefulness of data. Without that management, they become a detriment, not only to data management initiatives but also to the company itself. As a reminder, it is important that the three questions can always be answered.

Let's break down some functions and purpose within these platforms. Note that some of the terms might be seen as specific to a particular type of platform, but the term is not the important part of these examples. Regardless of the name, they are functions that should be accounted for.

Intake

When we talked about integration, we talked a bit about staging at the target. These platforms are targets. The intake function *is* staging as a function and the staging area is where it resides. The primary function of staging is to ensure that all of the data is received and accounted for in the target. This concept of staging is not unique to these platforms. Inbound staging is appropriate to all systems. One of the unique configuration parameters of staging is that there are no constraints on the data. This means that there is no configuration on the target side that will prevent the data from being written as received. Configuration constraints come in many forms including, size, format, data type, and character set. Any one of these could cause data to be dropped, truncated, or even fail the integration.

Failed integration might be the easiest to detect because the other constraints may appear to the integration solution as though the delivery was successful, when something was actually dropped, modified, or corrupted. It is appropriate to take the entire topic rather than filtering on entry. *No* modifications should be made to the data while entering or while in staging. This is essentially as close to a replica of the master as possible if appropriately designed, implemented, and managed.

Another characteristic of staging is that its purpose is to facilitate the intake so the storage of data is temporary. Temporary does not mean seconds, but I believe that it would be hard to justify anything longer than seven days and even that is a stretch. The more robust the controls and monitoring, the shorter time the data needs to be available for recovery. Once the data is persisted and backed up in the next stage, there should be no reason to retain the data in staging.

Raw Data

The raw data is the unmodified data from the master. It is not updated, it is not restructured, and it is not filtered. This is essentially the longer-term storage of the staging area. Why not just use staging? That answer should be obvious just based on the principle of not more than one data function per location. The data from raw storage might be accessed by the next steps more than once, where the staging area is one time and done except for emergency recovery. The performance of the staging area is important while the capacity of the raw data storage is a significant consideration. These two considerations alone can cause conflicts if attempted in the same location. There are other considerations but the evolving technologies may change some of them, so we will stick to the functional needs. It is possible that there may be some significant processing on the raw data during the movement to the next step.

Refined Data

Refined data is the resulting next step after the raw data. Refined data has had some level of processing applied to make it "fit" the platform and the business needs. There can be a wide range of processing including formatting, filtering, and structure. The processing that most internal uses require makes sense to do in one place rather than at each of the endpoint consumers within the system. The refining process likely creates the "master" for the internal usage of the data for various reporting and analytics use cases.

Some may wonder, "why not populate the refined data directly from the staging area?" I have seen it done but one of the reasons for separating staging and raw has been pointed out; the staging area needs to perform and not have undue processing attached to it. If refined data needs to be reprocessed for any reason, the raw data would be there but the staging data would not, so keeping the processing consistent makes sense. Another reason would be the data consistency between raw and staging. If they are both processed from staging how do you ensure that they are both fully processed before moving on? There are ways but it adds another level of complexity. Simple, repeatable, and consistent is always better.

Depending on the type of processing, it is possible that the refined data set is a unique data topic specific to the reporting and analytic use. We will discuss more detail of the "rules" around data topics in the methodology section.

Summary Data / Metrics

This might be considered part of the refined data depending on how the environment is configured. This also fits the reusability of calculations and doing them in one place so they are consistent. If an endpoint needs a different metric or rollup, there is still access to the refined data that is not summarized.

This is a good point to discuss the "I'm special" concept. Many people believe that their needs for data are unique and special and are different than the rest of the company. It is seldom true, and using commonly and consistently defined metrics will prove much more valuable to the company as a whole, rather than everyone creating a unique but "similar" version.

Marts (Functional Endpoints)

The term mart is going to have a specific function and design meaning to some people, so I want to explain that I use this term loosely. Regardless of how you design the solution, what you call it, or how many layers it has, there is a need for segmented users, processing, and data beyond the raw and refined data. This may be organized by function, by organizational structure, or even by users. There may even be layers of this data by function or users within these segments. Regardless of the structure, the function, subsequent copies of data, and new results, they exist.

This is where what most people see as the "real" work happens. The great reports and the analytics that produce projections of the future, or answer "why" from the past, come from this "working area". All the work and stages that happened prior to this should have been quite structured and managed with the purpose of providing this area with the best and most useful data.

Because this area is segmented for different purposes and new ideas arise every day, it is more difficult, or at least requires a different approach, to keep tabs on the data. Remember the discussion on data lineage? Data lineage not only applies to integration between systems, it applies just as much to systems that replicate data internally. It is very possible in large platforms for this purpose that there are hundreds of copies of data. How do you answer the three questions about all of them? They can be answered, but not without planning for the management and creating a framework to support it.

The Inevitable Default Master Source

As much as it has been stated that these platforms should not become a master source for a data topic, it is almost inevitable. It makes sense, therefore to walk through the situations that may cause this and the mitigation that might be applied.

Someone responsible for a master source will inevitably say, "They have it, I don't need to keep it" when referring to one of the larger reporting platforms. This sets up a reporting system to be a failure at being a master because it was not designed to be a master and, in some cases, no notification was given that they were now the new master. The reporting system should only need to be responsible for the data in the context of their use. In addition to not being an appropriate function for a reporting and analytics platform and all the issues that it can cause, some platforms are not technically designed to fill the availability and integration requirements of a master source. The default master situation can happen when the master system needs the data for a year for their purpose, but other systems need it for much longer. We will address this further in the records management chapter, but the prospect of a reporting platform becoming an unintended default master is an important consideration that all should be aware of.

In addition to the age of the data, there can be a circumstance where change history may "seem" irrelevant to the operational system. There are many potential examples of this such as price, customer names, customer address, item descriptions, inventory, and the list goes on to any data that can change over time. Depending on the design of the operational function of the data, some functions might require history and some may not. Privacy laws might require some history.

There is the operational need, the legal need, and there is the analytic desire. There seems to be a growing pattern of desire for unlimited data with the increase in "data science". Some would say that you can never have too much data or have it for too long. I have heard some say that and some recognize that it is an exaggeration. Finding the balance of need and risk is critical to managing the data and this perspective has a direct relationship to records retention, which will be covered in the chapter on records management.

The Creation of a New Master

When the output of your reporting or analytics creates very reusable data that is not available elsewhere, you have likely created a new data topic that needs a master location that meets all of the requirements of being a master. We will discuss the criteria for a new data topic in more detail in the methodology section of this book, but new reusable data does not mean a simple merge or addition of values. If $a+b=c$, c is a new value but as long as people know what a and b are, creating c is a very reliable formula that does not constitute a new master source for c.

Assuming that it is a new topic, it needs a home. Before having a new home and being a new master, it needs to have the appropriate metadata and governance approval to be a master data topic. Whether this is in an entirely different system or a different functional area of the same system, it needs a place with the appropriate controls that meet the expectations of others. This may be a shift in process and responsibility that people are reluctant to sign up for. When people realize what it is to be a master source, many may not want that responsibility.

A simple example of that is an end-user with a spreadsheet that many people have found to be useful data and it is not available elsewhere. Many people are very willing to share that information and feel a sense of pride that others find value in their work. Let's recap a likely sequence of events:

- In this example, the person created the spreadsheet for their own purpose, not to be a master record for someone else.
- They are very willing to let others benefit from their work, so they set up a location to share the results with others.
- It is set up as a group-share so they are not aware of all the people that are using the data or making copies of the data.
- This person gets direction "from above" to immediately change the formula used to calculate a couple of values in the spreadsheet because their need has changed. Of course, they do it because they are doing their job and taking direction.
- It is not their job or responsibility to even remember that they shared the data, know who is using it, or notify them that it has changed.
- Now everybody using the information based on the original understanding of the meaning has data that is just plain *wrong* in their use of the data.

135

The end-user spreadsheet example is used because it is probably easier for people to accept that it happens, but it happens in all types of non-master sourcing of data including the large platform reporting and analytic systems. It may be that it is especially there. If the source is not a master, they have *no responsibility* or accountability for what the consumer thinks the data might mean or for notifying them of changes.

In this scenario, where the sharing of the spreadsheet is acting like a master, it is not meeting some of the most basic functions of a master for that data. The data is being "shared" but not in all forms required for the business. The metadata is not being maintained in a consumable way. The governance process was not utilized to create new data and manage the metadata. A spreadsheet is not going to meet all of the distribution and availability requirements for a master, so let's assume that this data is moved to a true "system" that can handle the integration and availability needs. The management of change to some critical metadata still lies with the creator (the capture point) of the data. That is the only place that will be aware of the new meaning, based on the new formula. That is a responsibility that cannot be ignored when providing data to a master.

Let's take this example one step further to a specific column in the spreadsheet, which is the equivalent of an element in a data topic. The column heading is quarterly regional sales. Everybody knows what that means, right?

- Does everybody have the same definition of region in the entire company? Some may consider a region by those locations reporting to a regional manager. Some may see it as a geographical segment. Even if everyone sees it as geographical, the company restructured regions three months ago, so which structure is in this element?

- If there was a restructure, did the source "back-populate" the data for the new region to the beginning of the year or even further back?
- Is the quarter based on fiscal quarter or calendar quarter?
- What about sales? Are sales gross revenue? Do they include both paid and unpaid orders? Is it a net amount considering margin? Does it include returns? Does it include discounts? Does it include manufacture promotions or incentives?

You may think that the answer to some or all of these questions is obvious and it would be wrong for them to mean anything else, but that is the point. You *think* that. If it is not documented as metadata, I can guarantee that different people will have different definitions of what the data means because of their personal context of the words used in the label. This is only an example of a specific element but it can happen with most data.

I want to remind you again that this is not specific to end user spreadsheets. This type of scenario happens across systems. We are in a chapter on reporting and analytics and have spent a lot of time on the creation of a new master. The reason is that it is inevitable that reusable data will be created and it is therefore important that creators of the data understand the responsibilities and ramifications of creating a new master. It is not something that most think about. A report or analytics as an endpoint does not present all of these complex issues. It is still important that the people using the report understand the meaning of the data, but that is isolated to the scope of the report and not everything downstream.

Here is a very simple conceptual diagram indicating an appropriate basic flow of data to a new master from a reporting and analytics "ecosystem":

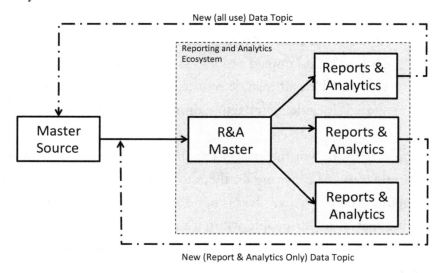

Figure 9-1

This diagram introduces a few new concepts as well as reiterates points already made. One new concept is the idea of a reporting and analytics master, which may seem contrary to the principle of only sourcing from the one authoritative source. As the principle has been stated so far it is, but we need to address the practicality and realistic approach as part of the logical implementation. This example should not be used to justify daisy-chaining data or using this pattern in places other than within a reporting and analytics ecosystem. This perceived exception is better stated as a clarification. The principle of sourcing applies to "system" sourcing of data. It is a reality that copies of data will be made internal to a system. This is sometimes done for technical reasons, for separation of function, or for user segmentation. Again, this is *within* a system. The best that can be done, in that regard, is to avoid the internal system daisy-chaining and this diagram supports that concept that all internal uses of the same data come from the same place.

Another new concept or term is the ecosystem. I am also going to call this unique to reporting and analytics. We have been using the term system a number of times and we will get to a more robust definition in the section on methodology. For now, consider the reporting and analytics ecosystem to be potentially made up of multiple systems that are coordinated for a sole purpose of reporting and analytics. You might also consider this to be a platform.

The *sole purpose* is important and is reflected in the diagram. There is no data flow from the ecosystem to any system outside of itself other than to provide newly created data to a new master. There are two new data topic dotted lines in Figure 9-1 and they represent the two functional uses of the new data topic. If the topic is only to be used within the ecosystem, it flows to the reporting and analytics master through the same intake process that it would from an external master source. The importance of that is to apply all of the same processing, controls, and management to the data regardless of source. The reporting and analytics master data can only be provided to consumers internal to the ecosystem.

The other dotted line populates a new data topic in a master outside of the reporting and analytics ecosystem. This is done when the data topic is needed by a system outside of the ecosystem. Both dotted lines should never exist for the same data topic. If the new topic is needed for other systems as well as reporting and analytics, the reporting and analytics master is populated from the "external" master. If you were only looking at the need of reporting and analytics, this might seem like a complicated path but from a complete data management perspective, it simplifies the total solution by implementing consistent and reliable methods. The path of data is much easier to follow and utilize management protocols that are in place and it makes change management easier when needed on a broader scale.

Clarification of Large Platform Reporting and Analytics

This chapter so far has been mostly about the large data platforms used for reporting and analytics. There is good reason for that because they can be part of the solution for getting data management and risk under control if appropriately managed. They are also a large somewhat concentrated risk.

All of this may make it seem like large platforms are the only place where reporting and analytics take place or the only ones that are important to data management. That is absolutely not the case. They present a different management problem so they are worth calling out, but there are other methods of reporting that are important. If the only place for reporting was the large platform, it would imply that all data needs to be moved to one of these platforms.

System Specific Reporting

There is some data that is not required to be merged with other data for reporting (primarily operational reporting); that can often best be done from the master source. In these cases, consideration is often needed to be given to the operational nature of the system with the same concept of not performing multiple functions on the same data in the same location. Depending on the size of data and the type of processing being done in the master system, this is often addressed in one of two ways. One is to have a unique location within the same system to use for reporting, so as not to impact the operational function of the data. The other is time separation. This is not the most robust solution but can work for operations that only run constrained hours, and reporting can be done in the "off hours".

Calling out this type of reporting supports the integration principle of not moving data unless it is required. If the data in the report is not required elsewhere or to be merged with other data for reporting, reporting in place reduces the risk of movement of data and can consistently produce higher quality output with less risk.

End User Reporting

From a consumption perspective, large platforms contain a large volume of data, but there are a set of data consumers that provide far less opportunity for controls and many more locations that could be difficult to find. To be clear, this is not about the reports that end users run on other systems, this is reporting created locally by copying data to their computer.

End users will consume data from wherever they can find it. Making their life easier is likely the most important criteria for many. The assumption of quality data is prevalent. If it's not quality data, then it's at least good enough. They likely know of someone else using data from "there", so if it's good enough for them it must be okay. Even if they don't know someone that is using it, why would the company have data that is not acceptable? I am running through these scenarios like people actually think those things, when they probably give it no thought at all other than they need data and they found a place to get it.

This presents the obvious risk of not sourcing from the master. The consumer has to assume that they know what the data is and there can be elements of the data that are missing or modified, making the results of their usage completely *wrong*. I am sure it would not be a surprise to you that many of your business decisions are based on a spreadsheet or data that someone put into a slideshow from "someplace". This data is presented as fact. One of the primary reasons that this happens is the expectation of speedy delivery without the appropriate data management framework to facilitate it. It is a common perspective that data management slows delivery rather than facilitates both speed and accuracy. The push, pull, and perceived contradiction between control and freedom exists for a number of reasons. This can include attempting controls with no authority, focus on control with no consideration of usability, lack of funding for a framework, and many other things. An obvious important aspect of a data strategy is to account for *both* control and efficient usability.

How Does All of This Relate to the Three Questions?

All forms of data management relate to the three questions. Here is a list of a few things that we have covered:

- Sourcing from the master increases consistency, which promotes the integrity of the *what* and the *meaning*.
- Reducing the number of steps and the number of copies impacts all three questions.
- New data and a new master may be required to preserve the adherence to the principles that promote the ability to answer all of the questions.
- Internal system data lineage is important to maintaining the ability to answer all three questions.
- Reusable processes promote the consistency and maintenance of the data, as well as increase the efficiency of the usability. Efficient usability reduces the complexity and the probability of solutions that circumvent the ability to answer the questions.

Reporting and analytics is all about the usability, which is the outer ring of Figure 5-1. We have recognized that the outer ring is not always an endpoint and that the what, meaning, and location may be impacted by the activity in the outer ring. Movement of data that enables the usage always impacts the *where*, but we also outlined the scenarios that impact the *what* and the *meaning*. These are still the same three questions and the same small set of principles that apply throughout.

Summary

Reporting and analytics is about using the data to create conclusions, whether it is reporting or deep predictive analytics. That is the function and purpose, but from a data management perspective it is an opportunity to simplify the environment, increase the consistency of the data, and create a framework that both respects data and enables its use.

This is not achieved without planning and dedication. A *significant* amount of your company's total volume of data is likely dedicated to reporting and analytics. I believe that you might be surprised at how high that percentage is if you were able to inventory your data. Just knowing that data has this purpose enables many functions and future requirements simply due to the fact that it is reporting and analytics data. We talked about ever-changing privacy laws and this information could be critical to that approach and compliance. The usage pattern is simply different than operation or compliance archive data. We also talked about a consideration for anonymization, and the master location in this type of ecosystem is one of the places where it could be implemented in a way that would have a very broad impact.

Reporting and analytics platforms are in a unique position to have a significant positive impact on data management. Unfortunately, many of them do the opposite.

Chapter 10-1

METHODOLOGY – WHAT IS IT?

This section has been referred to a number of times in this book up until now. This methodology, like the rest of the book, is not technology specific. It is also not a *complete* data strategy. It is not *comprehensive* data management. So, what is it? This methodology provides the *means* to address data management, data governance, records management, privacy compliance, and, yes, to answer the three questions.

Data is specific and its integrity is critical. Likewise, the understanding of terms, approach, and measurements of data management are critical. You cannot implement such a broadly impactful and encompassing strategy as data management without people being on the same page. I have seen a lot of statements that are intended to get people on the same page, but everybody has their own interpretation of what the terms in the statement mean. The terms used are so ambiguous and subjective that there is no way there can possibly be alignment that leads to success. You might say that this methodology, in part, addresses the means to communicate. We started some of these discussions earlier in the book, such as what is meant when you say data. Without that clarification, as basic as it may be, some people will eliminate some data because it doesn't fit their understanding and definition of "data".

In addition to getting people on the same page with the terms and concepts, there needs to be support for an approach to managing data that is achievable and can grow over time. If you look at terabytes, petabytes, and beyond of data, it is not reasonable to expect every conversation about data to either be about *all* data or about each individual element of data. One is way too broad and one is so small that you cannot have a realistic discussion about strategy or implementation.

How is defining terms a data management methodology? Terms alone are not. You need the terms, the relationship between them, and the usage models for all of them. These concepts impact and can benefit every aspect of data management. They can also provide a mechanism to segment data into layers or groups of data that enables achievable goals for managing data.

We have talked a little bit about some of the terms including data domains, data topics, and the master authoritative source. We have also talked about their importance in answering the three questions. We laid out the sequence of dependencies beginning with the three questions and adding respect before getting to the usage of the data.

These examples are more than terms; they are concepts. They are concepts of more than just communication. They are concepts of strategy, implementation, and measurement. Let's bullet these out:

- Communication
- Strategy
- Implementation
- Measurement

We will circle back at the end of this methodology section to ensure that we have covered all of these concepts.

In order for these concepts to be effective, they need specific rules of implementation. Consistency, as in the consistency of data, is extremely important to the success of this methodology. If you use a term such as data topic, it needs to be very clear what it means, what it can include, what it cannot be, and the impact that it has on your design, support, and the overall integrity of your data.

This methodology is designed to be implemented "as you go", but you have to start. The implementation of the methodology can grow in breadth and in depth. One area of data may focus on breadth and another on depth and the methodology works for that. It is essential to the success that flexibility exists. The rules are pretty rigid and because of that allows for the flexibility to plug things together in pieces of different sizes, at different levels, and at different times. Some benefits will be seen immediately but the real power of the methodology shows when the efficiency breaks through and eliminates steps in operations, project work, data discovery, and all types of maintenance including hardware, security, and the data itself.

Throughout this section we will pull in previous information and expand on its rules and usage. In doing so, various data management practices will be used as examples.

This is a diagram depicting the rough outline of the data hierarchy related to the methodology:

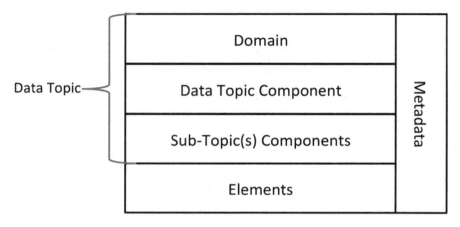

Figure 10-1

Most of these terms have been mentioned previously, but now it is time for a deep dive into their structure, relationships, and how they impact the overall data management effort. This is not the only way to depict data in your company, but we will start here as a foundation with a focus on the master data source and then move on from that.

Chapter 10-2

METHODOLOGY – DOMAIN

We are starting at the top of Figure 10-1 with *domain*. We talked about data domains in both the Strategy and Data Governance chapters. You probably have some idea that they are large groupings of "types" of data but maybe not much more than that.

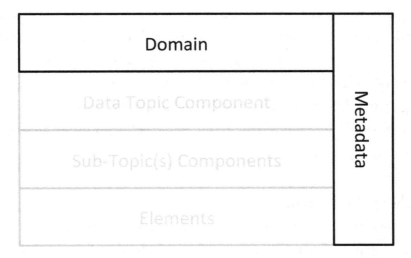

Figure 10-2

Definition

Across various definitions of *domain*, you will find a consistent word, and that is *area*. Other descriptors are territory and region. All of these have a geographic implication to them, but that is not required. The other thing that they have in common relates to what is contained in a domain and the idea that a domain is "big". So far, in this context, we would have a large amount of data that has something in common. That's not too earth-shattering.

Data domains have another specific technical definition when talking about data elements, but that is not the use that we are looking for. In a previous chapter, we started with data sets and evolved to data topics. Is there another term that we could use for domain? Let's get back to the definition first. The purpose of the data domain is to break the company's data into large chunks. They act as a container for data topics and they represent major business functions. A key word is major.

Now we have a definition that looks like: *a logical container of data that represents the major functions of the business.* This is the answer to *what* at the highest level. What "type" of data does your company have?

That works for me as a short definition but is domain the right word? I have seen data subject used, but GDPR used data subjects to mean people. Every word that I have looked at seems to have another meaning unless we move to something more verbose which could be as long as the definition. It seems that sticking with domain is just fine. As has been stated with other labels, the label is not that important as long as everyone knows what it means.

Building the Domain

This level of data many have some standards within your industry that could be utilized. Sometimes large industry specific data warehouses have "subject areas" defined. A subject area, or whatever your particular technology calls it, is likely very similar to what you will need for a list of domains. If you have something to use, by all means do so as long as it fits your actual need. If you do not find such a readily available set of domains, you will need to start from scratch.

It may take some time but you need to start. I would expect that you may find the need to make some modifications for a few months after you start as you find that two domains have consistent overlaps or you find that there is little to no use for one. Your list of domains needs to encompass 100% of the data in your company. Purely by that one requirement, the domains are going to have to be quite broad in their function. I would start with the concept of working toward a total of around 10 domains for all data. This is just to give you a sense of how big the domains might be. The difficult part will be to find the balance between not having so many that they are hard to maintain and not having so few that they are meaningless. If you start with a statement of what your company does in one or two sentences, you will probably find the majority of your domains within those sentences.

I will start by giving you a few ideas for domains that most companies will have:

- Reporting (and analytics)
- Products and Services (things that you offer for sale)
- Customers (but this is one that you might put to a higher level depending on your business model and number of other domains)
- Finance
- Legal / Contracts

This is obviously a sampling but a company is likely to contain all of these and others. Finding the level to put these might seem challenging but if you try to keep your number of domains to no more than fifteen, and I believe closer to ten would be better, it will help in understanding an appropriate level for the domain. It is probably going to be harder to make sure you have covered all of your data. Think about not only the business functions, but how useful it might be to have a top level name for a type of data if you were looking for it. Imagine you are looking for financial data and want to see all of the data topics in that domain and follow that logic for all of the domains that you are thinking of. Do they still make sense?

If you have built your data governance roles, you can certainly enlist those people and look at the structure of the data governance. This can be somewhat of a chicken and egg scenario since a domain lead is a key role in data governance. You might think that domain leads would 100% align with the domains in this methodology. It is ideal if they do but do not stress over it if they don't. It is also possible that the operational process of your data governance may drive data ownership of a data governance domain to cross data domains. If you have the opportunity to match them, and it makes sense to the structure of the data, do so and let it help you define the naming. It is not a hard rule like others that might be expressed in this methodology.

Rules / Guidelines
- We'll start with a guideline that was mentioned in the section on building the domains. There should be no more than 15 domains but closer to 10 would be better. Manageability and logistics will become an issue if there are too many. It is also likely to more closely align with data governance domains. An example used was customer and it was stated that it might be raised to a higher level. This will depend on your business model. If you have a primary focus on customers and have a lot of them with a lot of data about them, it may make sense to be the domain level. It does not hurt however to move it down a level if you have a small amount and have other types

of people relationships. Some may put vendors, suppliers, affiliates, and other business relationships all into the same domain with customers. This is art not science, but keep it manageable, consistent, and logical in order for people to know where the data might reside. If customer is not the top level, you will still be able to find the data.

- The second guideline is to keep the name short. It will have a long description attached but the label for the domain itself should be short as it will likely be used in a "composite name", as you will soon see.

- In supporting good data design and coding practices, give the domain an ID. This is far more important with data topics but can be useful here because the domain name could possibly change as you evolve but the ID will not.

- Use a term for the domain that means something within your business. It is the top layer of all of your data.

- You should do all that you can to avoid a domain titled Miscellaneous or Other. These labels serve no purpose. Do not give in to that temptation.

- The domains, in total, must encompass *all* data in your company.

Associated Metadata

We already mentioned an ID and a description. The ID is easy. The description should be more than a short description. It is okay to have a short description if you also have a full description. The full description is worthy of the size of something along the line of a one-page document. It should describe how it is a major function of the company, what the function actually does and list examples of the next level data (data topics) that would be contained in the domain. These are examples rather than an explicit full list that would cause maintenance of the document/data. The idea is that when someone reads the description that they would have an idea what type of data would be found in this domain and why.

There will be relationships to data topics contained in the domain, but that is really relationship data that can vary where and how it is stored depending on the structure and design of the repository.

The domain may have an owner, a date created, and a date last updated, but the metadata associated with the domain level is actually quite limited compared to the next levels. This is really just the basic context data that gives the value of the domain some meaning.

If you look at the three questions, the domain is the beginning of answering *what*. The related *meaning* is the small amount of metadata that we just reviewed. And the *where* is wherever you decide that your metadata for this data structure is going to be maintained. There needs to be one authoritative master for this data. This applies to all levels of metadata within this methodology; one place for all levels. This data, just as with any master data, cannot be maintained in two or more places.

Implementation Relationships

Data governance has been used as examples a lot in this chapter because of the domain label. Data governance certainly needs to understand the data hierarchy, which starts with the domain, but their scope of responsibility does not need to be the same as the domain. While it is easier if it is, forcing the match is not realistic. Here is one example of that scenario:

- Let's say that you have a customer domain and a legal/contracts domain. If the contracts domain name is simply *contracts*, it would also include customer contracts. It may be that you want to align the customer data governance domain with the customer contracts and that is okay, but the data would logically still reside in the contracts domain. This is probably preferable to changing the name of the contract domain to be non-customer contracts. Any domain name that does not have exclusions in the name should reasonably be expected to contain everything that fits the name; in this case *all* contracts. Going down the path of exemption naming can be a very slippery slope.

Because domain is such a high level grouping of data, it is difficult to draw broad relationships outside of data management and data governance other than the business and technical departments that might associate themselves with the domain names such as legal and reporting. Domain is important but also the most simplistic of all the layers.

Chapter 10-3

METHODOLOGY – DATA TOPICS

Data topics are the heart of this methodology. We will spend the most time on these layers. I say *layers* because we will address the data topics, data topic components, and sub-topic components in this chapter.

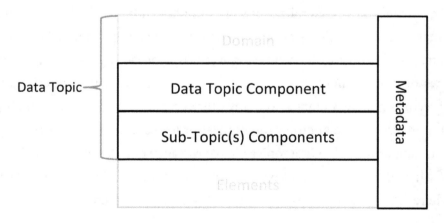

Figure 10-3

Some might even refer to this as the Data Topic Methodology. The reason for the domain is to understand the types of data you have and to provide a place to put common data topic components. The reason for the elements in this structure is to clearly define the contents of a data topic. The elements are the "real data" but there is no precise way to talk about them other than individually, which is rarely the conversation level information and is too complex to manage all aspects of data management at that level.

The Need for Data Topics

This brings us to the real power of the data topics and that is to provide a mechanism to not only talk about data but to clearly and precisely manage data at a level above the individual elements. Without this precise structure you are left to talk about individual elements, all data as a whole, or make general references such as sales data or customer data, which has no precision. There are certainly times that the individual elements are the appropriate level of discussion and management, but to manage or discuss all data at that level would be insanely burdensome and set you up for failure. Likewise, there are times when mass generalizations about data can be made, but they are usually general policy statements such as respecting data. Managing data, implementing a strategy, governing, measuring compliance to laws or management goals, responding to subpoenas, implementation of records managements, and many other activities cannot be reasonably and precisely done at either the highest or lowest levels. This is the gap that data topics fill. Data topics enable the answer to a manageable level of what, the meaning, and where. The data topic level is the only place where the metadata of location should need to be stored.

Definition

In the chapter on master data management we talked about evolving from the term "data set" to data topic and why that was important. We talked about the topic being used to reference the "topic of discussion". We said that the purpose of putting a label on a group of data elements was to give the grouping some meaning and context. That is more of a *why* rather than a definition. Let's start the draft definition with: *A logical and functionally operational grouping of data from a single source.* That covers some basics but we need to include "rule-based", or something like that, in order to get to the importance of the precision in its execution. We also need to include that it is governed to ensure the consistency of the metadata and its usage. Let's try the following:

> **data topic**: *A logical, functional, and rules-based grouping of data elements from a single source that is governed and maintained to ensure its appropriate usage and consistency of its metadata.*

This is a long definition but it covers the essentials of a data topic beyond just being a data set and it does not step into the *why* and *how* of the execution.

The Approach to Building Data Topics

Where do you start? As has been discussed, there are always two major approaches to the implementation of a strategy. One is everything new and the other is everything old. Everything new prevents things from getting worse and everything old starts to get your arms around your total environment. The existing items will need prioritization.

Obviously, a data topic starts with a domain and then adds the data topic component and sub-topic components. It is a good idea to have a layout of a rough structure of your data topic component-to-domain relationships, but it is not absolutely required and it will likely change some as you move through building data topics, and that is okay. Just make sure that if you change it dramatically, which should not happen often, that you update the domain description. This is one reason to be general in your structure of the domain. It is also possible that as you create data topics that you find that you are missing a domain. You may even find as you get further that you are not using a domain or that it is hard to decide between two, which might call for either a clarification of the domains or combining them. Iteration through data topic names and related hierarchy is far more likely in the earlier stages of building data topics and lessens significantly after the inventory of data topics has increased to a broader representation of the company. Before moving on to the rules and guidelines, let's make sure that the structure of a data topic is clear with the following diagram:

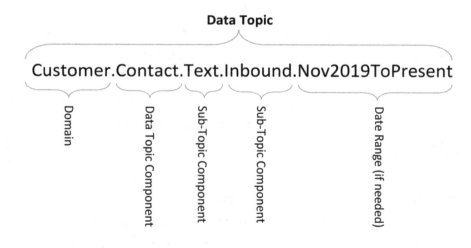

Figure 10-4

Rules and Guidelines

In order for data topics to be precise there are a fair amount of rules and guidelines. We will go over them one at a time and explain why they are required.

Rule 1: A data topic can have only one master authoritative source.

Before going into the explanation of this rule, I want to shorten up the naming of the One Master Authoritative Source to System Of Record (SOR). They are the same thing but system of record is pretty well adopted and understood. From here on out in the methodology, SOR will be used for this.

This rule is a hard rule with no exceptions. Splitting a topic across multiple source systems adds a great deal of complexity with zero value. A single source allows the topics to be used in conjunction with integration, data lineage, and other implementations. If two topics are needed for a particular use, then you simply consume two topics. This rule does not change an integration pattern; it simply allows the documentation and implementation to be both simple and precise.

If you think you have found an exception to the rule, you have not. Rather, you *may* have found the need for a new data topic. An example of one that you might come across would be the data being stored in one system for performance and operational needs for one year, but the data is needed by the company for 7 years so the remainder of the 7 years (years 2-7) are stored in a different system. This is a realistic scenario that is solved, not by sourcing the same topic from two systems but rather by creating two topics. The only difference in the topics is the date range. The date range can be one of the sub-topic named levels. It would typically be the last level.

There are never exceptions allowed to this rule! There is no justifiable reason to do so and creating an exception undermines the integrity of the methodology.

Rule 2: Data topics require an ID.

Through the process of building your data topics, it is inevitable that some data topic names will change. You will find related data that indicates that a restructuring of the name is relevant. The ID will never change. There may be elements that are added and that may or may not indicate a change to the name but the ID never changes. The names are important, but they are more like metadata for the ID that indicates the purpose of the topic and is one of the primary variables in the ability to search for data topics.

Rule 3: The data topic component and sub-topic component naming is hierarchical.

The total name of the data topic is the concatenation of the domain and all layers of the data topic components and sub-topic components. The most important aspect of the function, purpose, or ownership falls in the topic and the next layers further qualify the topic. Through all of the levels of data topic labels, there are some guidelines to determine the appropriate name, but there are no absolutes and your decision can potentially change as you add more data topics. Of course you want to try to get it right the first time, but by using the topic ID as the key, it makes it much easier to accommodate change.

The data topic component, just under the domain, should reflect the primary use and purpose of the data topic and be reflective of the next level of clarification under the domain. There are some domains that will have natural next levels. If you think of each level as drilling deeper and deeper into detail it may help. It might also help to think of it as a file structure, which it is not, that supports the same logical structure. Examples are likely to be the best way when it comes to naming in order to explain the guidelines.

In defining the domains, we talked about customer potentially being raised to a higher level. Let's say that was done and a label of *entity* was put on it. Customer would be a natural next level within that domain. If you raised the domain to entity, you probably had ideas of other types of entities that would go in the same domain such as vendors, trading partners, affiliates, etc. These would all share the same level as customer and the only thing tying them together in this structure is the domain name.

Whether you raised customer to a higher level or not, the next level of customer (the first sub-topic level) would be the same. The next level "examples" under customer might be labels such as contacts, purchases, demographics, user managed data, profile, preferences, and anything that fits the way that you track or manage your customers. Carrying this through to the next level, under contacts, you might have categories based on the media (phone, text, email, chat, etc.) or it could be that the next level is just the direction such as inbound or outbound. The volume and diversity of data can drive the level and sequence of the naming of topics. Consider the concept of wanting to search for all customer contacts. Having contacts below customer would allow for that. For that matter, so would reversing the order but that would probably not be logical unless your business is about contacts/communications. We will provide more examples as we move through this chapter. Again, this is not a rigid form that forces the label hierarchy but it is rigid in the structure.

Picking two topics that are the same but start at different domain levels would look like this:

- Entity.Customer.Contact.Inbound. Chat
- Customer.Contact.Inbound.Chat

As you can see, the only difference is the domain name containing the topic, but either way you can find the topic if you are looking for it. These examples might indicate that there is enough customer information being managed to justify customer being a domain level.

Rule 4: All levels can be individually managed and searched.

The data topic name is a concatenation of all levels, but each level needs to be able to be individually managed and searched. Creating the data topics without being able to find them does little good. The searchability and the ID that doesn't change, are two major factors that enable the flexibility of being able to change the naming as you grow through the process of building your inventory.

It is important to note that a specific word may show up in various unrelated data topic names at different levels. There are many examples of this. As per the previous example of customer contracts, if the domain is decided to be contracts, the next level might be customer. In this case, customer is also likely a domain name. Any given *component* name of a data topic is not unique. It is only unique in context.

This may seem confusing but it is powerful. You should be able to search for "customer" regardless of what level it exists in the name. You may also want to only search at one level, such as domain. While a word may show up in various topics at different levels, a word should not show up in multiple levels in the same data topic.

In addition to the flexibility of searching words within a data topic name, some metadata will be essential to include in search criteria. A good example of that would be SOR.

Rule 5: *A data topic is never a subset of another data topic.*

This is an easy scenario to spot or even script a test for. Let's use a few potential data topic names as examples:

Customer.Contact
Customer.Contact.Text
Customer.Contact.Text.Inbound
Customer.Contact.Text.Outbound

Of these examples the only two that exist at the same time and comply with the rule are the last two. [Customer.Contact] and [Customer.Contact.Text] are both invalid data topic names if the last two data topics exist. Even if the last two did not exist, the first two could not both exist because one is a subset of the other. Note that the domain is contained in the full name and domain is exempt from the rule because there are never data elements contained directly in a domain. The first level of the data topic will always have *at least* two entries or the domain would be inappropriate.

Another way to state and test for this rule is to say that once you are beyond the domain name, there should not be a single choice at the next level. It might be easier to show a diagram:

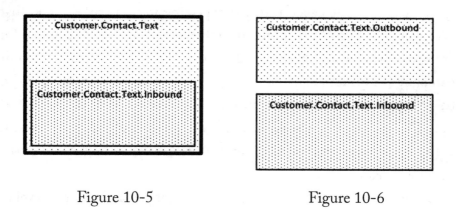

Figure 10-5   Figure 10-6

In Figure 10-5 the inbound topic is a subset of the [Customer. Contact.Text] topic. The data elements in the inbound topic are also included in the "parent" topic. That means that the data elements are inventoried twice. The [Customer.Contact.Text] data topic is therefore an invalid data topic.

In Figure 10-6 there is a clear separation of the two topics and the only data replicated are certain keys, which in this case would likely be something like a customer ID. The customer ID would not be "owned" by either of these topics but rather by something like [Customer.Profile].

The subset topic does not add value and adds a great deal of confusion. One of the reasons for having data topics is to inventory the data in the company and to be able to talk about data in a precise manner without talking about each element. In Figure 10-5 you know that the topics are in the same location so it adds no value there either.

Taking the example a level up, the same rule applies. [Customer.Contact.Text] is a valid data topic name, but if that was the complete data topic name that was directly associated with data elements, neither the inbound nor outbound topic would be valid. [Customer.Contact.Text] with nothing in the level below it would be an appropriate place to put data, but you would likely assume that there would be other topics at the same level as text, such as [Customer.Contact.Phone]. You might create just one level called text first expecting to fill in others, and that is okay, but until you add more, the only types of contacts accounted for are texts. This would likely get flagged in a periodic review. If your company's only method of contact with a customer was text, there would be no reason for that level because the data would be at the next level up. This is currently labeled *contact*, but *contact* could also be replaced with *text* as based on that company scenario, it would be the end of the data topic name.

One more way to look at this rule is that if you add another level to a data topic name there must be (or planned to be) two or more labels at that level and there are no data elements associated with the level above it.

Rule 6: Data elements are unique to a topic.

This is a broader implementation of Rule 5. The subset of data is unique, but common data even across data topics is a risk. In general, you should find a data element in only one data topic. The purpose of this is to avoid creating multiple variations of data topics that may not only be subsets but partial combinations across data topics. There is one exception to this "rule"; the keys to other topics are allowed. They are actually required. In a simple example, if you have a SKU in a sales transaction, that same SKU is going to be in the product information, inventory information, supply chain information, and more. That data element will show up in multiple data topics and it needs to. However, the data element can only be "owned" by one topic, as we will discuss in the section on data elements. This "exception" for sharing the keys across data topics is not really an exception but rather an expectation. Because of this, the statement "except for keys" could be added to the rule.

However, there is an actual exception that is not approved but can be expected in existing data. This does not make it okay, but it is important to understand that you will likely find this type of data and know how to address it. While I do believe that you will find them, they are hopefully not widespread. Regardless, it can be addressed.

This exception situation is where a system has consumed data from one or more other systems and then added a few elements to that data, and then is acting as the source for all of the combined data along with the new data that it created. We have talked about the idea that simple merging or simple repeatable functions do not constitute a new data topic, but the daisy-chaining of data through different systems with a little data added is bound to have happened. The *rules* of data topics are a great way to help find those instances.

There are some usage models that will push this concept. It would be far cleaner to avoid them but since there will be such a push, it is best to be prepared for them. They may show up frequently in integration design models. Integration models out of analytic environments and "lake" environments are even more likely. This does not change the patterns that were discussed in the integration chapter; it only changes the data contained in the integration.

The general argument is that forcing consumers to consume 5 different topics when they only need five elements from each of them rather than the 100 in each one is too burdensome. There is some logic to that but there is complexity that is often ignored. You still need to know where all of your data is. One answer could be that you move all tracking of data to the element level which should be available through your lineage solution, but do you now need to track all data that way in order to get back to the master? Just the concept of combining five different topics gives a strong indication that the system providing that is not the SOR for some or all of the five topics. The SOR is still critical and we know what happens when you move further from the master.

I can think of probably a dozen different example scenarios and multiple ways to "solve" for each of them, but that point alone indicates that it is going to get more complex and you cannot have dozens of solution patterns and still expect to manage the data. So what is the answer to this scenario? I will give you a couple options and you will need to decide which one or two (or one of your own) you think you can *consistently manage* and still be able to answer the three questions.

1. You list all data topics included in the integration with a single integration source. The data topic with an integration line does not mean that the entire topic was consumed, so this is a method to still see the possibilities rely on the lineage for the details. This does not break Rule 6 but it likely breaks an important rule of only sourcing data from the SOR. If this system is the SOR for all of the data topics, it might be that the data topics for that system are not appropriately defined.

2. You create a new data topic that includes the aggregated data. This does break Rule 6 and adds to the complexity of the inventory and traceability of data. You can "soften" the breaking of Rule 6 by considering every element that is not unique to that data topic as being a "key" to another data topic. The master source of that "key" is then tied via the data element metadata. This is a stretch of the "key" term but this is an exception and exceptions break rules. One thing to keep

in mind is that when creating a new data topic, it is still a "copy" of data and the use of copies not only adds complexity, it also adds risk.

3. If you look at the two options so far, the common theme is that copies of data are being used. Copies of data are supposed to be an endpoint. A unique pattern for SOR and integration was defined in the chapter on reporting and analytics. It was applied to a reporting ecosystem. If you broaden the use of that ecosystem SOR you could allow for reporting use-cases outside of the ecosystem. This does not remove the need to track the data but provides some level of control of the source and of the usage of the data. This would not apply to an operational system as a target for operational use.

As you can see, these all add a level of complexity and are clearly exceptions to multiple requirements that are in place to allow for the management of data and the ability to answer the three questions. If you do not address the situation by either not allowing it or finding a consistent and manageable exception process, your data management objectives will fail. You will not be able to answer the three questions with a documented level of reliability.

Rule 7: Date Range is the last sub-topic component:

When different ages of the same data topic are in two different systems, the date range of the data should be the last sub-topic component in the string of the complete data topic name. This allows for the identical data topic name, up to the date range, to exist in two systems. It does not break a rule and it also provides complete search results and clear expectations of what data would be found in each system.

When setting the date range make sure you don't use actual dates, unless it is historical data of a retired system or on a "data hold", instead provide the range such as "creation + 1 year" or "years 2-7".

Rule 8: *Do not use the name of a system at any level of the data topic name.*

The system is required metadata but it should not be part of the name. The data can change systems, but the more important reason is that a system is not a data function or data definition. As we discussed in the chapter on data governance, it is important to purely look at data rather than at a system for its function and meaning.

Rule 9: *There can be no duplicate data topic names.*

Even though the ID is the unique key, preserving the meaning and integrity of the name is essential. The name will be used in searching, not the ID. The name should not be reused even if the topic name is retired.

Guideline 1: *Base the contents of a data topic on the functional and operational use of the topic.*

You might question how much data to put in a data topic. There is the rule that you are building the topic from a single system, but how do you decide what goes in the topic? Some will be obvious such as an invoice. Every element in an invoice needs to part of the topic. There are topics, however, that might seem to all be related data yet the usage follows very different patterns. If you find that situation, look for the high volume of usage. If 95% of the users/consumers of the data use 20 elements of 200 elements that you are considering, it is probably a good idea to create two topics. One topic contains the 20 and one contains the rest of them. If the scenario was changed to a total of 25 elements, it would make sense to keep a single topic. Also, if the consumers of the 20 elements were 50% rather than 95% and 50% used most of the elements, then I would leave it to one topic.

Splitting related data in a single system should not only be based on the usage but also on the preponderance of usage. Keep in mind Rule 4 that does not allow for subsets of data topics.

Guideline 2: Don't use plurals in your names.

This will not break anything if you do, but there are a few good reasons not to use them:

1. Almost everything is plural so plural is implied. Example: Customer (I doubt that you have just one).
2. Encourages consistency. If you occasionally use plural, you may find yourself with the same level having both text and texts when they are intended to be the same thing.
3. It simply takes up space. A data topic name that drills down 5 layers or more can get pretty long and extra characters can make a difference to readability.

Guideline 3: Consider a maximum goal for the number of levels in a data topic name.

You could find yourself trying to get too granular and this consideration may help. I have worked with some pretty complex and large environments and I have rarely, if ever, found the need to go past 5 levels including the domain name, and 3 or 4 is very common. If you absolutely need 6 it would not break anything, but I would consider it strongly before going to that level.

Guideline 4: Be consistent with the location of company or brand labels.

It is expected that some companies will need to address multiple companies or brands. This data clearly needs to be captured, but where do you put it? The only "rule" is to be consistent. There are pros and cons to different ways of addressing this. I will point out a few of those and you will need to determine what applies best for your situation.

If the companies are completely separate in management, personnel, and data (and are designed and expected to stay that way), keeping separate hierarchies in separated repositories probably makes sense. If you want to share data, personnel at any level, or anticipate the merging of even some functions or data, I would not keep them separate or you will have a syncing and consistency problem. As we have discussed, naming structures can change over time but consistency is critical.

If the companies have similar topics that would be named the same other than the fact that they are for a different company and potentially stored in a different master, the topic name needs to reflect the separate companies. The master location alone requires that the topic and its name is not the same. Also consider that people may want to have the flexibility to search for topics based on company or across all companies.

Where do you put the company distinction? Do you put it above the domain, in the domain, at the top of the data topics, at the bottom of the data topics, or somewhere in between? Each can have their own complications. At the top, either above or in the domain, sets up a very rigid and separate hierarchy for the companies. This might be too rigid for some. There is a reason to have the date range last even when dealing with multiple companies in order to allow for variations of SOR of the same topic over time. If you put the company last, then what about the date? The top of the data topic is intended to reflect the primary function under the domain. If you are looking for easy search capability, then a fixed position would seem to be a benefit. These are just things to consider. An option would be to put the company in the name at the end of the topic, except when superseded by the date. You could also add an attribute in the metadata at the data topic name for company. This metadata would not be visible in the name but would be consistently available for sorting and searching. You would of course need the checks in place to make sure that the company in the name and in the metadata is not out of sync. There are plenty of ways to solve this but, again, consistency is the key. If a company changes in some way, the ability to consistently filter or globally change by company is essential.

Similar to the example used in Rule 5, if company is used in the data topic name, there needs to be at least one more topic at the same level to represent the other companies. If there is no company, by definition, the topic represents all companies in scope for the repository. You may have a situation where there are ten companies and all of them are represented as the same topic from the same source except one. In this case, a company entry of "non-company x" at the same level with "company x" is acceptable and may be more efficient and logical than creating 9 more data topics. While exclusion naming is not ideal, it can be the most efficient solution for some situations.

Metadata

Note that the metadata, other than possibly the name hierarchy relationships, is stored in such a way that it is associated with the entire data topic concatenated string. This concatenated string is actually the data topic, and the data topic components and sub-topic components that we have been talking about make up the data topic. The data topic metadata may be managed by associating all of the metadata with the ID that represents the data topic string. The reason is to provide the flexibility of evolving the naming and hierarchy without disrupting the metadata, data elements, and all of the external functions associated with data topics. The following is a list of metadata that should be associated with the full data topic (ID):

ID – The ID is critical and the methodology will fail without it. All relationships to the data topic should be tied to the ID rather than the name.

System Of Record – This is the one authoritative master record of the data topic.

Location within the SOR – This represents the details required to find all of the data in the data topic. This could be table(s) in a database, or a URI, or whatever method is used to find the specific data in the data topic.

Data topic component/sub-topic component hierarchy – The representation that ties the hierarchy of the data topic name together. This can be done in a number of ways and it could vary depending on your repository design and technology. Whether you store the string or the levels, it can meet this requirement as long as each level is still searchable. This could also be done by storing each "parent" at each level, but there needs to be a consistent method to know at what level the topic is done and what the full name is. The design of the repository application just needs to meet the requirements and the design might alter some details of data storage.

Description – The description is not constrained in size but should not reference current system locations. The description is of the data topic function, purpose, constraints, comments about origin or process that created it, and any known gaps or flaws in the data. Some will separate gaps and flaws into a separate piece of metadata so that it stands out and is not missed.

Last modified – This could be just a date or also include what was modified depending on how your repository is managing change history. The changes are mostly likely to be in naming changes because any change to description, other than minor typos, may represent the need for a new data topic. If the functionality, source, or purpose has changed, a new topic is in order. Adding a few elements does not mean that the description has to change. Creating a new data topic implies that a data topic could end and a new one would "replace" it. That is possible in circumstances such as a change in the business model where the old topic is no longer used. That does not mean that the data topic is retired and removed. It would mean that it is no longer being populated. This brings us to the next two attributes of metadata.

Oldest and newest data – These are two points in time that may or may not be actual dates. The newest data for most data topics is likely to be "today". If the data is no longer being populated, it would be a date. The oldest data, depending on how you are managing records retention could be either a date or something like "today- 7 years". This is not the highest priority data, but as you see it capture it. There will be a need for it. Other initiators such as system retirements or records management may escalate priorities of some of this work.

Last reviewed – This is for maintenance. There should be periodic reviews of the data topics to ensure that the metadata is still correct and that the data topic even still exists. This might be considered an annual event depending on your company's processes and resources. This data does need to be maintained and it is generally not an onerous task.

All associated data elements – The real data that makes up the data topic. This contains the link to the elements and like other metadata, it is important to associate it with the ID.

Relationships

This methodology is not for the sake of documentation and not only for the very important task of creating an inventory of your data. It has real world benefits that increase as the methodology results increase.

An important point that has been stated multiple times is consistency. The data topic names and decisions made regarding those names need to be consistent. It is best, at least in the beginning, that one person or small group creates the names. This group should have direct accountability to the data leadership. It is likely that the Data Governance Office (DGO) is the appropriate group for that work. Even after the initial phase, I would strongly recommend that the review/approval stay in place for the data topic names and metadata.

Even with the rules in place, distributing the authority and responsibility for these decisions can lead to overlaps, inconsistencies, and disputes that can undermine the effectiveness of the data topics. This is not an onerous task to place on one group that understands the rules and the importance. It takes a very small amount of time.

Data topics have far reaching impacts on many processes. It might be more accurate to say that they *should* have. Data governance will use them and follow a rule that only one Domain Team can be responsible for any given data topic. Security rules might be applied at the topic level. Topics can be very good indicators of privacy law scope. Subpoenas are likely to be able to be answered by starting with data topics. Integration will use data topics. Data lineage will use data topics. Records management will use them and we will discuss that usage in the records management chapter. General consumers of data will begin to lean on not only the clarity of the communication of what a data topic means, but on the integrity of its content. Every aspect of data management can benefit from data topics. The idea of talking about the replication, capacity, frequency of use, quality, stewardship, retention, security, performance, etc. is much easier and more accurately done when done at the level of a data topic that has a precise meaning.

Chapter 10-4

METHODOLOGY – ELEMENTS

Here we are at the real data! None of the structure thus far matters without the real data. Before we take that thought too far, the data topics including domains, data topic components, and related metadata are all real data. They were just created for the purpose of managing the elements. The integrity of the entire stack is important.

This book started off with a discussion about what it means to be data. That discussion was at this element level. Even the discussion of data governance was mostly talking about the element level.

Let's look at where the elements sit in relation to the construct of a data topic.

Figure 10-7

There is no reason to explain why we need data elements because it is *the* data. Every data element should eventually be associated with a data topic. There will be a number of opportunities that will present themselves to define the elements and most of those opportunities are greatly enhanced by a good data governance process.

Now that we are deeper into the methodology, let's step back a little into data governance. It is data governance and a method of documenting the element metadata into a metadata repository or data catalogue that are going to be great triggers to ensure that a data element has a home in a data topic. The more data topics that are defined, the easier the association of new data elements becomes.

Our discussion of data governance to this point has been about data elements and that is appropriate. It is also true that the relationship between data topics and data governance is important in the context of data elements. Unlike data domains that can be split across multiple Domain Teams, a data topic is assigned to one Domain Team. That team is responsible for the metadata of the data elements as well as the data topic.

Since the data topics are based on the functional grouping of data, it is logical that a function would align with one primary Domain Team in data governance. Primary is important to this logic because others will always be interested and have use of the data, but the ownership and responsibility needs to belong to a single body. That is why it is important to compile comprehensive members for the Domain Team. Also keep in mind that others will likely need to be involved in the creation of data topics.

As reviews come into the data governance process, they will likely come in at the element level, but there is work for data governance outside of the requests for new data elements.

New elements are a trigger for data topics, but there are a number of other triggers that can come from data governance. As we discussed, the workload of data governance can come from the new data as well as getting control of existing data. Existing data might be prioritized by most used data, most used system, most inconsistent data, or most requested data either through privacy laws or subpoenas. All of these examples benefit from having a container of data topics for the data elements.

We discussed the metadata regarding "data" at the beginning of the book as being at the element level. This chapter on the methodology has added metadata to other levels of the data. Because we are adding the elements into data topics, there is one additional piece of information that is useful at the element level:

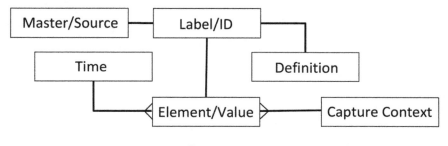

Figure 10-8

179

This diagram should look familiar, as it is the same as Figure 1-2 with one exception. The "Master/Source" has been added. We have already stated that the location is stored at the data topic name level so why a source here? The vast majority of these elements within a data topic will default to the master location of the current data topic. Remember a rule in data topics is that the elements within a data topic are to be unique to that topic with the one expected exception of "keys". These key elements are mastered elsewhere and this new piece of metadata is the pointer to that master source if it is different than the current data topic. All of the other metadata of the key element *must* be inherited from the master source in order for it to be a legitimate key.

We have made it to the bottom of the data topic stack and have all of the layers assembled but there is more explanation needed of the methodology. There needs to be more clarity for usage and implementation.

Chapter 10-5

METHODOLOGY – SYSTEM OF RECORD

The term of SOR has evolved within this book from one authoritative source, to master source, to system of record. They are all valid phrases regarding this matter. The term "of record" is equivalent to "one authoritative", and "master" is "system". The term "source" is quite vague and "system" seems a bit more descriptive, and yet I believe without clarity there would be very different perceptions and opinions on what a system is.

As with other aspects of this book, consistency is the most important. Regardless of the definition, clarity is needed in order to have all consumers of data and practitioners in data management on the same page. The "of record" part of the phrase is easy but the system needs definition so let's get to it.

The definition of system is not easy and there are a lot of different opinions, but we can't leave it there. I have gathered input from hundreds of people and have been in some pretty heated debates so I know that it is not easy. However, if you do not have a position there will always be confusion and miscommunication. Let's walk through a few of the experiences and discussions that I went through and share some conclusions that have been drawn.

One of the most prominent assumptions is that a system is the same as an application. That may be, depending on how you define an application. Applications are purchased or built, so do you define an application by how each vendor licenses their product? That would not seem to be too consistent because some will write a license for their application being equivalent to their brand and just "add on" functions or modules for a higher fee. You could end up with half of your company or more being one application by that definition and not every company works that way. We *need* consistency in order to use a SOR as part of our data management strategy.

We need to determine if there are aspects of a SOR that can be considered requirements or ones that *cannot* be used to define a system. Since our context is data, we can determine that data is required for *our* purpose. This would mean the system would need to store data in order to be a system of record. However, there are those who would dispute this because it is an application that is running and functioning that needs support and if it's not a system, what is it? Maybe it's still an application. No conclusions yet!

Also, based on the need for stored data, maybe the system is defined by the repository that stores data. For example, any "application" that writes to this database (or any type of repository) is a system. What if an application writes to multiple repositories or if multiple unrelated applications write to a shared physical database using different schemas? So far, there are more questions than answers and that is going to continue for a bit.

Similar to repositories of data, some would say that it is determined by servers. It is absolutely true that more than one application can run on one server and it is also true that a single application can run on multiple servers. Then add the complexity of virtual servers. Servers are clearly not the answer. We can even take it far enough to conclude that servers *cannot* be a factor in determining a system.

Stepping out to various dictionaries, they all use a variety of similar words, but one consensus on a system seems to be that it is multiple parts working together to accomplish something. That really doesn't help much in this regard.

So far we know:

- The dictionary doesn't really help
- It cannot be defined by servers or repositories
- It cannot be driven by applications because purchased applications may be defined differently by different vendors
- It needs to persist data in order to be a SOR

Let's explore that last one a bit. While SOR has a particular meaning for the purpose of data management, there are others that will likely need to use the term for other purposes. We know, for example, that a SOR needs to persist data, but what is something going to be called that meets all other criteria except that one? They are still likely systems so that needs to be considered in the search for a system definition. Suppose a leader asks the IT support team how many systems they support in the company? Then the CEO asks someone else. Then the CTO asks how many applications they have. I can pretty much guarantee that all answers are going to be different. It is time to get on the same page and be specific about systems and applications, as well as types of systems. I think from this, we can reasonably conclude that we may end up with different types of systems. The different types of systems will be helpful for more than just the definition, as we will explore.

We have been very broad in our definition of data and that is appropriate, but I would guess that when most think about data, they are not thinking about application code, configuration files, or monitoring data. We are talking about types of systems but the types of systems have types of data that will likely drive the types of systems.

When we talk about data governance and the business driving the meaning, it has been inferred that we are talking about "business data" and not IT operations data. Those are two obvious distinctions that that can and should be managed with different considerations. There are some details that are important. All systems with business data will also have IT data so the distinction becomes the purpose of the system. We need one further distinction that is going to be very important. We have talked about reporting and analytic systems and their purpose. They essentially should only have data whose purpose is reporting and analytics, and the vast majority of it is copies of data from elsewhere that are already accounted for. Most of that data will be business data, but it is certainly possible for a system to be aggregates of IT data for reporting and analytics.

If we conclude that we have three types of systems, does that cover all data and all systems that we could encounter? They are all very broad types and we have defined them as being their *primary* purpose. Is anything left? Remember to separate the master records concept from the type of system. A system's primary purpose is driven by its primary function. Is it a business function, an IT function, or a reporting and analytics function? I believe that you would be hard pressed to find a system that does not fit into one of these types. You could possibly find yourself feeling that a system is equally split. In that case I would suggest the following priority:

1. If business is at least equal function of a system or if it is the SOR for *any* business data topic, it is classified as a business system. This does not include a data topic that is created for internal use to a reporting and analytics system. See Figure 9-1. It does include systems that have IT monitoring and logging and systems that also do reporting. It is almost a

rule that a system has to be the SOR for at least one data topic in order to be a business system, but I can think of one exception. There are systems whose primary function is a business function, but they only store data for minutes, hours, or days so they cannot be a SOR. They are still business systems. There will likely be very few of those.

2. Reporting comes second. Remember that reporting can be on either business data or IT, or both. Regardless, if the primary function is reporting or analytics, it is a reporting type system.

3. The only type that should be left is IT systems. You may call them something else, but they are likely created and managed by IT for the purpose of IT management and operations. Some of these systems may contain copies of business data such as backups, logging, and monitoring but the purpose of the systems are IT operations and not as a source for business data. System types are not driven by copies of data.

We now have systems typed but we did not conclude the definition of a system. Understanding the types may, however, aid in coming to a definition. We know that a system has a functional objective. The components within the system are unified in their objective. There is likely more that is unified. Considering the operational use of systems and the support context of systems might give a clue. If systems run independently and are maintained separately, they are not likely part of the same system. If one system is "down" another system should not be down because of that system failing. To be clear, this does not mean infrastructure such as server failure, nor does it mean that the dependency on the missing data from one system causes less functionality of the other system. It is more likely that they actually share "run-time" code.

If the code fails, the "system" is down. Everything that fails because of that "run-time" failure is likely part of the same system.

We have already determined that servers do not determine a system but let's take that further. Adding servers or even deploying duplicate code for the purpose of performance or availability does not constitute a separate system. It is still the same functional system.

If we put all of this together in some sort of summary fashion, we should have a definition for a system:

System: The combined components of applications that have a common function and are unified by shared application code.

As you can see, we ended up in a place where data is not even mentioned in the definition. That aspect of it comes into play in the "of record" portion of the phrase. The system definition also covers systems that may not be a system of record. We covered a lot of territory to get to the definition of a system and mentioned a number of rules along the way. This definition should work for all roles that care about systems, but if it does not, it gives you some idea of what will need to be addressed to come to a consensus. Worst case scenario if a consensus cannot be reached, you will have to agree on different terms to use because you cannot use the same system term and have it mean different things. The rules that define it are important.

The system was the more difficult aspect of system of record, but let's make sure the rest is covered. We stated earlier that "of record" was the equivalent of the one authoritative source. Now that we have an idea of a system or the considerations for your definition of one, we need to outline some considerations for how to determine the appropriate SOR. You may find it obvious in some cases, but in other cases you may find that representatives from different systems will insist that they have the most accurate data and are therefore the SOR. In other cases, you may find that nobody wants to admit to being the SOR and take on the responsibility.

We know that SOR refers to the master record or the one authoritative source for a data topic. What are the criteria for determining the most appropriate system to be the SOR? We have covered most of the requirements, but let's review. The SOR:

- should be as close to the system of capture/creation as possible. Many times it is the same system but if not, it should be the next system.
- is responsible for the integrity of the data. Integrity covers a lot of area including quality, completeness, and security.
- is responsible for making the data available to consumers by the means required to meet the business needs.

These are only three requirements, but they are big responsibilities. Remember that this is where it all starts and the management and governance is prioritized to the SOR because that is where the metadata is managed.

In determining the most appropriate SOR, the ability to meet the requirements is the first step. You will likely find that the most appropriate systems may have "owners" that resist being the SOR because of the responsibilities. You may also find the situation where people will claim that there are multiple valid sources for the same data. These people may or may not be the system owners. We have discussed a number of reasons why that is not a viable answer. This is an opportunity to get to the real SOR by asking a few questions:

- Are there any obvious differences in the data because comparing the two sources would likely prove, at best, to be very difficult and time consuming?
- What is the reason for more than one? Is it performance, ease of access, or even "appropriate" data? You will be surprised what

you find by asking questions. Some of the alternate sources of data are referred to as "convenience" copies. That statement includes the word "copy". That answers one question.

- A very telling question to ask is, "if you find a difference in the data which system is right?" Some will push back on this question and say, "they won't be different." They will be, but just stick to the question of, "okay, but what if they are?" Most of the time people do know the most appropriate and accurate source.

If the reason for not using the most accurate system is a technical reason, one of two choices need to be made; either the technical issues are solved or the SOR moves to a different system. You cannot have two (or more) SOR for the same topic. If you hold to these simple rules, the integrity of data and the ability to track lineage increases exponentially.

Remember the diagrams in the integration chapter and the observation that the documentation of integration provides very obvious exposure to the use of alternate sources of a data topic once the data topic SOR is identified. It is important to understand that the use of an alternate source of a data topic is an intentional and willing use of data that should be expected to be of less quality and susceptible to changing its meaning over time with no notice. Some will say that this SOR business is extreme and an exaggeration. It is not. I have seen it over and over. It is simple; very simple. It may just be different than how things work today. A SOR can and should be easy to use for those that have an appropriate use of the data if the correct SOR is identified and appropriate design and processes are in place. You can spend the time meeting the requirements in *one* place or do it partway on two, or three, or more systems with little consensus of accuracy, increase in complexity, and create a significant challenge in the ability to answer the three questions.

Chapter 10-6

METHODOLOGY - OTHER DATA SLICES

To begin with, what is a slice of data? I am hoping it is obvious but it is a term that might not be frequently used and you don't need to use it if you choose. I choose to use it to bring a unique view of the concept to this particular case. A slice, in this context, could easily be called a category, a type, a classification, or other terms. As with other concepts in this book, the major importance is not the term, but rather the understanding of its meaning and the concepts that it represents.

We have walked through the hierarchy of data from domains, through data topics, and to the elements. We have talked about the systems and types of systems and their general functions as they relate to managing data and other operational aspects. Earlier in the book, we talked about integration, daisy-chained data, and reporting and analytics platforms. These concepts are all relevant to managing data and the methodology of data topics. Together they imply a categorization of data that has not yet been explicitly defined.

There will always be many ways to slice data for different reasons, but the first one that I want to address is a particular set of categories into which all data falls. This slice of the data is best done at the complete data topic name level. We just talked about business, reporting, and IT being categories of systems and those are also indicators of the type of data that you "might" expect to find, but they are about system functions and not explicit to data. To make the assumption that all data topics in those systems are of one "type" would be a mistake.

We know that we have been talking about master data in the SOR chapter, but what other data is there? There are copies of data. Copies of data are most easily tracked and discussed at a data topic level. Data lineage tooling and processes enable that identification at a topic level if appropriately configured, *as well as* the element details. When the data topics quantity increases and the lineage data is available, you will be able to start to get an idea of the landscape of your data. Copies of data can exist in any type of system. You might figure that reporting and analytic systems are the predominant place for copies. They are likely a significant portion, but by no means the only place. Copies of data can end up anywhere, and they do. This is why the master vs. copy concept is a different slice of data, but does master and copy cover *all* of the data? Not quite. There is one more concept to cover in this slice and it might sound like a system type but this is different. It is reporting or more precisely reporting and analytic results.

Copies of data may exist to be used as copied, but often they are created in order to create a different set of data. That different set of data might occasionally be handed off as a new master data topic, but often it is the endpoint. In that case it is not a master because it has no consumers (other than people) and it is not a copy because it is new data. It was likely created from a copy or copies, but the result is something new. You can put a label of reports or reporting and analytic output or something to that effect on this type of data. This applies as well to the internal master referred to in Figure 9-1 that never leaves the reporting and analytic ecosystem.

In regard to copies of data, the end-user storage of data is potentially massive in your organization. You actually have no clue of how much, where it is, or even what it is used for. This category of data is big and complicated enough to address in its own chapter. The pre-read on that chapter is that there is no silver bullet but it cannot be ignored. It is still company data that your company is responsible for.

Now that we have data sliced by masters and copies, what are other slices of data that are relevant? I am not going to try to list them all, but I will offer a reminder of a couple that we have already touched on. There are slices of data by privacy impact. Those identifiers of data that may be impacted at both a PI and PII level, as well as any other regulations that your industry may have will help in being compliant with those laws. Some of those regulations may benefit from data topics or other slices of data and some may not. It is important to understand and document the various slices that are being used in order to maximize the opportunity for sharing and enriching all of the efforts.

Another slice that we have talked about is security classifications. Again, some security classifications may align with some data topics or other slices of data. A privacy law is likely to intersect a security classification for example. It is of great benefit for those that define and manage the slices to understand the other slices. I cannot emphasize that enough.

One final example is the slices created by records management. The benefit of aligning records management with data topics has already been stated, but records management will likely have their own slice. Records management will create expectations on retention of records. In theory, there will be a number of rules (slices) about the retention of data. For example there might be 1 year, 5 years, 10 years, etc. Whatever the rules are, there is likely a finite set that will apply to all data and all data topics. There may also be some intersection with the copies of data referred to earlier.

I could go on with more examples, but your organization will create their own. The major point of this is to be in the loop with all creators and managers of these slices of data. Collaborate with them in order to share the benefits derived from the intersections and as well avoid redundant slices.

Chapter 10-7

METHODOLOGY – IMPLEMENTATION

We have walked through the concepts of this methodology, but in order for it to work it has to be more than just words on paper. Where do you start and how do you do this? The answer is not really any different than how you have to implement any methodology that involves change. We have already discussed the importance of the appropriate leadership and authority and the need for a data management strategy. Those are essential so we will try to stick to just the specifics for this methodology.

Education

There are some terms and processes that will be new to the organization so education is essential. It is important to focus on how this methodology will impact individual roles, so that people can see themselves in the methodology. It will likely impact all roles in some way and some more than others. Education is, of course, important for data management as a whole, and this methodology and its terms should be included as you communicate your strategy and talk about the three questions. The terms are important and I have offered you my perspective of some of the terms, but it is more important that you use consistent terms and that people understand them. You will find that there are variations of terms amongst practitioners, vendors, and tools that operate in this space. That is why the definition is more important than the label, but in order for you to communicate and manage effectively internally, you need to be on the same page with your terms.

In this entire methodology there are a few key lessons for all to understand. The use of data topics is something that most people will easily accept because they currently talk about data in these general terms today. They will talk about customer profiles or sales or inventory data. The push, and it is not a hard sell for most, is to understand that those terms probably need qualifiers that make up a complete data topic in order to be specific. For example, you might use [Finance.Sales. US.Retail.Gross] as a name rather than just sales. This might not be the labels you would use or the order that they would be in based on your business model, but even by the naming it is quite easily understood that just saying sales is not enough.

The other extremely important concept is *one SOR for a data topic*. It is important that all users of data understand the benefit of a SOR and that it provides not only a simplification of data management, but greatly improves the integrity and reliability of the data that they use. Many users will not be interested in how it works or participate directly in data management, but everyone can have an impact on the success of the methodology used to implement a strategy. These two concepts are amongst the easiest and most important concepts to convey to the masses. You may be surprised how rapidly these concepts are adopted. People need to talk about data. The people that manage, secure, maintain, and govern the data need it, but everybody that uses data needs a way to communicate their needs and most will appreciate that someone is looking after the integrity of the data they use.

Starting the Methodology

One of the many significant benefits of this methodology is that it will work regardless of where you start. Where you start is going to be driven by business priorities and short-term needs, but the methodology will help to ensure that the work is reusable and sustainable. You may find that you need to make modifications along the way as you progress and learn more, but it is designed to be flexible enough to allow for that.

We have mentioned some likely triggers for starting data management initiatives and they all apply to this methodology. It could be privacy law compliance, data governance initiatives, some particular area of data quality concern, or data management being applied to new projects. Regardless of the trigger, you will likely find that the triggers are looking for answers to the three questions, and having the ability to answer the questions with a consistent format and at multiple levels of data will prove very useful. When a project or a court subpoena is looking for data, they might request a few specific elements, but more likely they will ask for a "type" of data which equates to one or more data topics. Having defined topics, a documented internal process, and a verified SOR adds considerable credibility to the data.

The data triggers might come in the form of specific data elements or at the type of data, but regardless it is your opportunity to do one of two things. Ideally you have completed the topics and list of elements that meet the need of the request and the ability to answer the question of what data is available (and from where); that can be impressive. Even if you have not yet touched that topic, this is the opportunity to define a topic, the SOR, and at least some of its elements.

Identifying only some of the elements is valid. You do not have to complete the list of elements in order to create a data topic. You do not even need to define *any* data elements to create a data topic. There is still value in the association of a data topic to a SOR. It gets people to the right source and using common names. The elements will fill in over time. Integration solutions are a good source of opportunities to populate elements.

The creation of new data needs to find a data topic home through the data governance process. The existence of data topics built from a "document" such as a receipt, or invoice is a good opportunity to complete data element association to a data topic. Other than existing well-defined topics, such as documents, it is possible that the only way that you will know that a data topic list of elements is complete is when you get to the point of doing a complete system inventory. There are some system owners or business drivers that will want to prioritize a complete data inventory on a system. This puts every data element in a system into a data topic. All data has a home. A way to shorten that is to not let the sprawl happen to other systems by only noting that particular data elements are copies from elsewhere. Most systems will have some data that is copied from elsewhere and it is not necessarily part of a data topic in the system being inventoried unless it is a key in the data topic. Refer back to the element section of this methodology. System decommission is another event that could trigger this initiative to find data that can or must be kept or deleted.

Short of accounting for all of the data elements, a similar activity can be done to identify all of the data topics in a system. Again, the focus would be on the data topics for which that system would be the SOR. This activity is usually best handled by an interview process that requires both IT and business involvement.

Many people, especially IT people, will likely think this about data so they will expect or want to talk about the data as it relates to a database or other repository. That is not where the discussion needs to be. The best way to pull out the data topics in a system is to talk about the system's functionality and what people use it for. The only thing that I would caution in this regard is to not go too big in the scope of a data topic. Remember the rule: *A data topic is never a subset of another data topic.* This means that if you defined the data too big, you may need to either reduce the scope of the data topic that you created or "retire" it and replace it would one or more other topics. This is really not as hard as it might seem and it is not a disaster if you miss; it is just something to try to avoid. One way to avoid it might be during the interview process to ask about the various "types" of a particular data topic.

When you have a data topic in draft, ask if there are multiple types of that topic or if they are all handled/processed the same. Even if there are multiple types, if they are handled and used in the same way, then it is likely safe to make it one topic. This is also a good example where having both IT and business involved could be beneficial because the business might see it as all the same, but IT may know that part of the topic is processed in a different way.

This process should be able to be completed at the data topic level with 90% accuracy in one to four hours. Four hours is the extreme for the biggest and most complex systems. Most systems should be able to be completed in one to two hours. In order to achieve this, you need the right people in the interview meeting. If you can't get them, it is probably best to postpone the meeting. Experts in the support and use of the system are important and so is the diversity, especially across IT and business. These meetings can be very enlightening! You will find that people are doing things with data, making assumptions, or have beliefs about the data that are simply not true. It is *very* useful.

You started the process with the domains and vetting the highest level of types of data that your company has. From there, you may have been looking at just data topics without elements or the need for elements creating data topics, or likely a little bit of both. As you go through the process, you will find sweet spots that are "easy" and sweet spots that are highly recognizable in their benefit. You cannot do it all at once. It will take time. There is a lot of data, but this methodology gives it a flexible structure to preserve your work and create value and reusability.

Tools

We did mention tools briefly and also have made the statement that this approach is technology-agnostic and it is. That does not mean that technologies are not needed to be successful, to scale the process, and create reusability. We just mentioned preserving your work and creating reusability, so let's start there.

Outside of the tooling needed for managing the data governance process, this methodology will benefit greatly from three types of tools. It may be that two or three of them are actually contained in one vendor's offering. This is where the technology-agnostic concept comes into play. I would only caution on being tied into any vendor's proprietary solution. The solutions need to be flexible to meet *your* needs and the structure of this methodology, as well as generic enough to be portable if you should want to extract your data for other purposes or to change or enhance tooling. Those technologies do exist.

I am going to start with two of the tools because they are closely related and have a codependency. These are a data catalogue and a data dictionary. I offer them separately because there are tools that only do one or the other and some that do both. Separate is fine as long as they can share information. By sharing information, I do not mean copy it from one system to another, but rather that the end user will likely need to traverse from one to the other seamlessly.

Both of these tools are quite simple in concept, and you may find tools that boast of lots of bells and whistles and doing everything for you. As mentioned before, be cautious of that. A data catalogue simply needs to store the inventory of your data, whereas the data dictionary stores the definitions and context of your data. This is where the definitions and interactions can get a bit fluid. You might, for example, store the definitions of the domains and data topics in the catalogue, and store the definitions of the elements in the dictionary. The location and/or reference to location and hierarchy needs to be available functions of both.

If you look at these tools in the context of the three questions, the *where* is assisted by both because both physical location and hierarchy aid in finding the data. The meaning of the data element is certainly in the data dictionary and at a higher level might be contained in the catalogue. *What* data you have is in the catalogue. This also means that the tool that is likely to provide the most benefit in finding the master data is going to be the catalogue. This adds the search requirement.

It should be pretty clear why the interaction and interoperability of these two tools is essential to making the data operational. It needs to be easy to store when you create it, and it needs to be easy to find when you want to use it. Remember to account for the levels of the data topic creation and the ID as the key to the complete data topic when you are purchasing or building a tool. Yes, building a tool is an option.

That gets to the third tool and it is almost entirely about the *where*. This is the lineage tool. The lineage tool should be able to track the movement of data topics as well as elements through your enterprise. The element level will indicate whether some elements have been eliminated from the data topic so you will have the detailed information of where. Another function of the lineage tool can be to trigger the evaluation for new data when a data element is modified. Some types of modifications would not modify the meaning, such as a modification of structure to fit a new repository, while others would. Some types of modifications may be able to be configured into the lineage tool so that reviews are not triggered unnecessarily.

The catalogue and dictionary are focused on the SOR because that is where the data is created, defined, and distributed. The metadata follows the data lineage to new locations. If the data is modified to the point of creating new data, it triggers the new data creation process. These three tools can provide you the answers to all three questions when populated, but of course they don't populate themselves.

Using the Results

We have already mentioned that the impact is very broad, but let's take a brief look at a few specifics.

End users and project work will reap great benefits from being able to find the data that they need. This may seem simple, but I would bet that if you could add up all of the hours spent on projects finding data you would be very surprised. They don't know who to ask, so they start down the path of word of mouth and tribal knowledge and end up eventually finding data with no assurance that what they have found is the most accurate available. Using the methodology and tools not only saves time and money on the project work, but enables the almost untraceable benefits of accurate data implemented by the project. Identifying business impacts caused by inaccurate data will almost never be traced back to the project or the fact that they used the wrong data to begin with.

We spent a lot of time on integration and the impact can go both ways, but when there is a good baseline of data topics, integration can become much more automated, cost effective, and accurate. The output of integration can create or clarify element to data topic relationships as well as consume them. Integration is also a major player in the input to lineage.

We also spent time on privacy and various examples of laws and the idea of being prepared for the unknown. The answers to the three questions puts you in a position to respond to requests, laws, inspections, and litigation based on a method that has built a way to find data based on data topics, elements, locations, and meaning.

We have not talked a lot about records management, but that chapter is coming. For now, let's just say that records management is about managing "records". What is a *record* these days? It used to be that records were documents, and some still are, but what about the masses of digital data? What is a record? It is a data topic!

We could go through all data disciplines and show some impact to each, but when you start to combine this methodology with other processes that are in place, you will see how this methodology becomes core to unifying a practice of data management.

This methodology combined with security practices, architectural standards, record retention rules, data models, and integration design (to name a few) will present powerful and consistent means of communicating and understanding data management in a way that becomes part of the nature of business. Data topics and SOR become part of the common language. They are used when doing architectural reviews and are validated with a documented source that helps others measure success and provide a feedback loop for updates and improvements in the data and the process.

Of course, there will be those that will say that it does not apply to them, but the essence of managing data applies to all. As stated previously, those that just jump to usage and forget managing what the data means, its integrity, and its security (respect) do the company and the purpose of data a disservice.

Examples of various situations and solutions have been used in this chapter and other chapters throughout this book, but remember that they are examples and not an explicit confined situation of applicability. If you have a "different" company style, or different integration patterns, or different technologies, the requirements and concepts are still the same. You still need to be able to answer the three questions. You still need to respect data. And, you still need to make the data available after doing those things. Along the way, you should be able to communicate with each other and measure your progress toward a data management goal that puts you in a position of quality usable data. It's that "simple".

I don't want to leave the concept of measuring progress hanging. I can give you a few examples, but what and how you measure is almost limitless. You clearly will have counts of the number of data topics inventoried, number of systems of record touched, number of systems of record with completed data topics, number of data elements with complete metadata, etc. Those are important numbers and you can trend those numbers and more, but what does that mean to most people that are not directly trying to achieve that goal? Very little.

Your company's data strategy will need measurements and those measurements can be supported by the methodology. These include objectives such as reuse, integrity, cost, compliance, and other results that align with your strategy. Measuring the ability to answer the three questions is inherent to the methodology. Answering the three questions is a requirement for most objectives because, again, you have to know what you have, what it means, and where it is before you can do anything with it or set any standards for it.

How you measure *specific* strategy objectives can be unique to your company's strategy, but some common baseline data will likely be required in addition to the three questions in order to show and measure the effectiveness. Cost and time are probably two of those baseline components. These are not as straightforward as counts but they can be done. The cost of finding data, cost of maintaining data (both labor and infrastructure), cost and time to respond to requests, and many more methods of measuring are considerations. The quality improvement of data may be able to be measured where there are known issues with quality or consistency. I would also suggest tracking the new discoveries that happen along the way. These discoveries include things such as gaps in data or misunderstandings or discrepancies in what data means. Most are surprised by what is uncovered through this process. Much of that happens in the interviews conducted for the SOR data topics and in data governance at the element level. Some of these discoveries can be very significant to the point where some, including leadership, will find it hard to believe that it actually is true.

Some metrics will be simple and just require information to be tracked and recorded. Other metrics will require combining with previously defined metadata or with related efforts and cost such as project and infrastructure work. Some may require calculated reasoning and deductions. Whatever the method, agree on the metrics up front and much as possible so that the opportunity for capturing data is not missed. You will add some along the way as the maturity increases, but keep in mind that a good goal should be measurable. Happy hunting.

Chapter 10-8

METHODOLOGY – MAINTENANCE

As with any documentation or operational data, it will become useless unless it is maintained. This maintenance is primarily about the data topics. The domains will have little to no change and they will not be triggered by periodic reviews, but rather by finding that you are not using a domain, that you have no domain that is appropriate to a data topic, or that you have overlapping domains that could be combined. The data elements based on what they are will also be triggered by events rather than periodic reviews if appropriate rules and data governance processes are followed. Once an element's meaning is defined, it should never have any substantial change. A change to the meaning requires a new element or it will corrupt the downstream usage of the data. If it is a common practice in your company to "reuse" data labels because the data is already flowing to other systems, please stop that practice. What happens to the reports or analytics that were using that data? Are you sure that you know all consumers of the data so that they could change all of their reports to treat the different meaning of the element as two different elements based on dates? Just don't do it.

Data topics will need periodic reviews for a couple of different reasons. The data topic name is the most common communication method for talking about data; its integrity, its availability, and its consistency are critical to the adoption of the methodology and data management in general. This is really about maintaining the metadata of the data topics. If you cannot maintain the metadata at that level, how could you possibly expect to maintain your company's data?

Data topics will also encounter events that will trigger review or modification and that can be used as a documented review. This will likely happen more frequently in the first stages of your implementation as you find the appropriate naming and hierarchy of a data topic. New data topics may be created that are related and may cause a shift in the naming of existing data topics. This is why the data topic ID is critical because it will never change. The meaning may need to be updated based on scope of the topic but the functional meaning should not change. The mapping to data elements might expand; however, many of the data topics will not be touched by an event that forces an update or review, they will just be utilized and accepted as they are. When a data topic has not been "touched" for a defined period of time, a review is in order. This is a very short review but very important. The primary review points are whether the topic still exists and whether the SOR for that topic is still valid. You could argue, and rightly so, that these points of review should have been picked up by governance or some other form of review or change management. That is true. It will take some time for that adoption to make sure the metadata is updated based on change. This is why it is important, as with all data management strategies, to engrain the management of the metadata into existing processes, make them measurable, and back them with authority. Updating metadata is a very minor step in any process but a very critical one. As this process gains more adoption, the number of topics needing review will shrink and become a very routine exercise. This is the reason for the metadata mentioned at the data topic level that indicates when it was last modified or last reviewed. The periodic review would only apply to those outside of whatever time parameter that you define for reviews. Annual reviews should be fine for most situations, but your specific circumstance may alter that.

Because you have other metadata associated with the data topic, you can also parse out the work based on system, domain, governance team, type of data, or type of system.

A purpose of managing data is to provide reliable data and the purpose of maintaining the metadata is to provide a reliable process. If everybody does not have trust in the data and process because of invalid data, the process will fail and everyone will go wherever they want for whatever data they can find with no *factual* knowledge of what it means. And we are back to why we need data management.

Chapter 10-9

METHODOLOGY – SUMMARY

We have covered a lot of territory in this methodology section so let's recap and draw some further conclusions. The methodology outlined is based on the concept of hierarchical data topics that encompass a set of rules and guidelines in order to provide both structure and flexibility to your data management process.

The structure consists of domains at the top, followed by data topic components and sub-topic components, and ending in the data elements. The structure itself is not complex and one could wonder how something so simple could provide any value. If there were not rules and you just threw names at data, there would be no value and, in all likelihood, that is what most companies are doing today. The value in this structure is brought forward with the rules that are applied to the structure and each level of the structure. The purpose of the rules is not for the mere sake of control like some overarching and domineering government or dictator. It is to provide consistency and a means to be successful in this large undertaking of data management. The metadata and the rules provide a base from which to progress and to measure. Measure not just the compliance to the rules, but the progress and success of the data management initiative. Remember the purpose is to add value and the methodology is the means.

Rules

Let's review some of the rules:

1. There can only be *one* SOR per data topic.
2. A data topic does not encompass the scope of other data topics.
3. The data topic name consists of the domain, the data topic, and as many sub-topics as it takes to uniquely define the topic.
4. The data topic ID is the static value of the data topic and should be used for all external references.
5. A data element should never be repurposed. If it is a new function, description, or purpose, create a new data element.
6. Data elements should not be shared across data topics other than the keys to other data topics.
7. Data topics need to be reviewed and maintained.
8. A repository with search capabilities is required in order to make the information reusable.
9. As with all data management initiatives, this methodology requires leadership support and data governance that is measurable in its progress and value.

There are more rules and guidelines, but these are just a few of the highlights.

Structure

The topic structure looks like this:

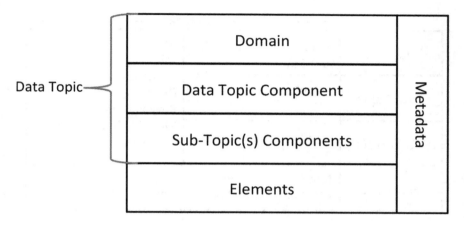

Figure 10-9

This is the same diagram as Figure 10-1. The structure is important for providing both the consistency and flexibility required. Each layer is unique, but we talked about the data topic, data topic component, and sub-topic components as one because the sub-topic components are just further clarification of the data topic component and the same is true for each successive sub-topic. There is no rule for limiting the number of layers, but it is good to impose a fairly hard "target". I have personally found that no more than 6 layers total, including the domain, is needed.

The domain is included in the full data topic name. Regardless of how you decide to concatenate the various levels into a full data topic name, be consistent with the separator or indicator that it is a new level. I have used a period most often, as in the examples provided previously such as [Customer.Contact.Text].

Metadata

While each layer is its own entity that can have metadata, the majority of the data topic metadata is stored at the fully concatenated data topic name, or the ID if you will. Let's take a look at the breakdown of the metadata.

			Metadata
Domain	Name Location	Description	ID SOR
Data Topic	Parent ?		Elements Definition Review Date
Sub-Topic(s)	Parent ?		Modified Date Company?
Elements	Name Location	Definition Context	Master Time

Figure 10-10

There can always be more metadata stored, but this should be considered the minimum for accurate and effective use of the methodology. The exceptions might be the items marked with a "?". The function of the metadata with the "?" needs to be accounted for, but may be done in a different way. The "parent" is just one method of creating the concatenation of the data topic name. It needs to be accounted for but there are other ways to do it. The "company" is one option discussed as a way to account for multiple companies in one repository, but there could be other ways. Even though you can add more, keep in mind that you have to maintain anything that you add. Do not add more unless you have the plan, process, and resources to maintain it. Incorrect and outdated metadata will be a detriment to the trust in the data.

The data topic component and sub-topic components are used in the hierarchy and are the building blocks that make up the data topic. I know that the term of data topic is used twice in two different contexts. You might think this to be an issue, but in this case the distinction of data topic components is going to disappear to the vast majority of people and just become the layers of the data topic name. The data topic refers to the string of the fully concatenated components that has an ID associated with it.

At the beginning of the methodology section, I said that we would circle back to make sure that a few key aspects were covered. These were:

- Communication
- Strategy
- Implementation
- Measurement

Check, check, check, and check. The communication was covered by terms and education initiatives. The data management strategy is serviced by the data topic methodology. The implementation details of where to start and potential alignments, and roadblocks were discussed. A point was made about various measurements and how they related to your data strategy and the three questions. More than these points were covered in the methodology section, but we have verified that the basic objectives have been accounted for.

There is one area that was mentioned about the implementation that may deserve a few examples. It was stated that combining this methodology with other existing data management disciplines could create an even more powerful and impactful solution. Some of this will happen naturally, but assisting the alignment can be beneficial. You will find that others not only use this methodology and its results, but will provide data and triggers back into the methodology. That interaction with others not only improves the quality and efficiency of the methodology for its consumers, it helps to engrain it into the culture of the organization.

We have touched on a couple of these interactions, such as the obvious data governance alignment and we will discuss more in upcoming chapters on records management and legal, so we will leave those for then. The way that your organization segments and operationalizes its data related practices will vary from others, but the point is to look for the opportunities.

Architecture is a broad term and can have lots of different implementations, but a few key architectures are integration, data, solution, application, and enterprise. This is not the total list and they are not going to be implemented in the same way across companies, but if you have them they will be reviewing or guiding architectural decisions. Most architectural decisions will directly or indirectly impact data. This is a key group of people to have on board with the data strategy and methodology. They will help to ensure that solutions are designed in alignment with the data direction and be able to notify or escalate when there are issues.

Security is another architecture but there are usually other aspects of security other than architecture that impact data. Security is, for a large part, about data. Security in general will have guidance and likely enforceable standards that can be measured. It is essential that the data strategy and this methodology consume and support those standards and likewise it is important that security aligns with the data strategy, the methodology, and the process. Measurements will likely be able to have some synergies as well.

I could go further into things like data modeling, application design, and other aspects of data, but the point should be fairly obvious by now. The alignment of these practices is beneficial to all and the best way for that to happen is with a comprehensive data strategy that understands and aligns all of these data related practices by design. We are still back to the three questions. You cannot do any of these things without knowing what the data is, what it means, and where it is. Keeping the environment in a position to be able to answer these questions is something that everyone should have as part of their objectives. The methodology provides a framework to ease the answer to the questions, record the results, and reuse the information.

The methodology provides the structure and flexibility and it is because of the rules that it can work. We have reviewed some of the rules and I want to emphasize that they are rules. I do not believe that rules are meant to be broken, but acknowledge that they will be. Any good rule has an exception process. An exception process needs to be consistent and documented. Exceptions are not new rules that allow people to say, "they did it, why can't I?" Approved exceptions should be rare and well documented. Exceptions do not eliminate or reduce the need to manage data. They make it more difficult and each exception needs its management plan that is different than the standard. There is a cost to this that should be considered with the exception approval.

Combine this methodology with the three questions and you have a mechanism to communicate, share objectives, measure success, and provide a structured simplicity that the masses can both understand and support.

Chapter 11

RECORDS MANAGEMENT

Records management has been mentioned a number of times in the book, but it is probably worthwhile to step back a bit and understand a little of the concept in general. Has records management become an outdated concept? Not at all. Has records management become and outdated term? Not if you allow the definition of record to keep up with the technology. I have seen some label it as records and information management, which might imply a broader scope than intended.

My first experience with records management and records managers was regarding paper documents. It might have possibly included microfiche. Records managers were in charge of the storage of boxes and boxes of documents. There were, and still are, companies whose purpose is to store the boxes or data and to shred them at the appropriate time. Depending on the type of storage and the type of contract, it would seem likely that in some cases that boxes were lost and the time and method of destruction could be in question as well.

The ability to manage boxes of paper documents is not the point of records management in this book. There are still paper documents, but the amount of data that is digital has surpassed the amount of paper and it is still increasing. The idea of keeping the "original" is diminishing as the original *is* digital, including things that were previously written such as a signature. In some cases the only paper copy is one that could be created from the "original digital".

The concept of what is managed has changed but the primary purpose has not. There are laws that require the retention, and/or destruction of certain documents/data within certain time parameters. There are contractual obligations and expectations set by your company. There is also the idea that there is risk in keeping some data for too long. The risk is not about doing something illegal, but rather that data is evidence regardless of its original intent or purpose.

This concept of data retention is partnered with data destruction. Some records management teams may use terms that convey a focus on either retention or destruction, but it must be about *both*. There are "camps" within your organization that will focus on one or the other, but finding the balance is essential. Again, I drift to the generic function of records management. Regardless of your organization's focus, there has been an evolution that has left some traditional records managers in a bit of an uncomfortable or undefined position.

Let's assume that the management of paper documents is covered. How do you transition that to the work required for data that is in so many places, with so many variations, and using so many technologies? It might seem to some records managers that they need to become technologists. I would say that is not the case, but they do need to understand some basic concepts in order not to be "run over" by technology jargon.

This book has stated over and over that it is technology-agnostic but not technology free. The requirements are the requirements regardless of the technology. Regardless of the terms that records management uses or the focus of their initiative, there is a shift from documents to data. A document has preservation, retention, destruction, and other expectations conveyed by the records management group. I don't want to oversimplify the paper documents, but it was certainly a more simplistic scenario. These documents go in these boxes, in this place, until this date, and then they are shredded. How do you do that with petabytes of data that haven't been labeled or defined and you can't find them? That is an insurmountable task that some will walk away from.

The information provided thus far in this book makes it very possible. Not only is it possible but the compliance to the requirements can actually be measured. *A document is a data topic.* It acts like a document and serves the purpose of a document. It has a functional purpose that is likely the primary criteria for records management rules. It is located and managed in a single location much like a piece of paper. One of the differences that is not minor is the ability to change the document. A document that was signed and put in a box for storage is unlikely to be modified. It maybe could be intentionally manipulated, but it would likely be an intentional effort to deceive. The respect for documents is somehow higher than data. Data can be and is modified to meet business needs, which is one of the alignments that many could agree on. Any data that has been modified has effectively destroyed the original "document". This is of course referring to the master record of that document and not copies that are intentionally altered and not used to represent the original.

There is the consideration that some data is intended to be modified and as long as that is acknowledged and part of records management, it is fine. It cannot be assumed that it is okay. It should also not be assumed that because it is modified the original does not exist. Take for example the design where all changes go to a reporting and analytics system. That system could overwrite the data that they have, but it is also very possible that the reporting and analytics system would create a slowly changing dimension that would contain all of the changes and history of the data. Does the original exist in that case? Maybe. If it does, where is the master? You got it; it is in the reporting and analytics system. Remember, all data has a master. If it exists, there needs to be one authoritative place to get it. In regard to records management and data topics, there would likely need to be two data topics with "similar" data but are known to be different. Go back to the implementation options for potential ways to address this.

We now have an expectation of retention rules, purge rules, and integrity concerns. All of these are still facilitated by data topics. Records management applies the rules to a data topic as they would have applied to a document. *Any* data can be defined by a data topic. We have covered the data topic concept enough to understand that *all* master data fits in a data topic and there are expectations around the copies. Let's stick with the master data topics for right now and then move on to the copies.

Every data topic should have a records management rule applied to it. In fact, all data should have a records management rule applied to it. What in your organization triggers the engagement of records management? Here is another opportunity to align processes. Records management cannot apply rules to the data without a data topic. I say that because a rule applied to something other than a defined data topic with all of the associated metadata is vague, open to interpretation, has no assigned owner, and is not measurable. Records management requires the answers to the three questions as well as data topics.

If you take your assortment of rules, assuming you have them, and apply them to data topics, you now have a records retention landscape that is functional and measurable. There is, however, one layer missing that can provide a much more manageable process; that is the "data categories" (records management slices of data). These data categories might have been referred to as document types or something of that nature in a "paper" records management process. My intent is not to tell you how to manage your records management categories and rules, but rather how to use data topics to facilitate the records management of data.

Let's say that you have an assortment of rules that totals 25. Many organizations will have less, but some could have more. You now can map those twenty-five rules to RM (Records Management) data categories. You then map each data topic to a RM data category. The data topic has metadata assigned to it including the SOR, so you now have a communication and documentation process that not only aligns to a records management process, but is greatly simplified and manageable.

What happens when one category of data has a change in the rule? It changes in *one* place and all requirements are up-to-date. Example: If you have a category that is called financial filings and the RM rule for those changes from one time duration (rule) to another, you just repoint that category to the new rule. All of the data topics associated with financial filings are then related to the new rule via the data category. I will step into another tool shortly that can even help in the automation of that.

To be clear about the rules that I am referring to, there may be many "categories of data" using the same rule and many data topics that are associated with a category. A rule is the expectation, rather than the method. Let's say you have an expectation that data is retained for 7 years and at the end of 7 years it is destroyed. You also have another one where data is retained for 1 year and then destroyed at the end of one year. You might have another that specifies that current data is kept for 5 years (meaning that there is an expectation that the data is updated without history). You get the idea. It is about the rules, regardless of what they are and why they are. You will likely have categories of data that are driven by laws, regulations, and the concern for business interest and liability. These categories are mapped to a rule as well. There are likely far more categories of data than there are rules. You can map the categories to a data topic and inherit the rule, but in the end most people are going to care about the results, which is the rule that is applied to a data topic. A diagram may help.

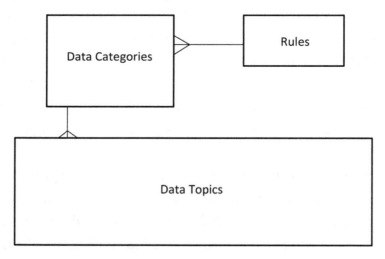

Figure 11-1

A rule can be associated with one-to-many data categories. A data category can be associated with one-to-many data topics. To put some perspective on the size of these, you might have 25 rules, you might have 100 data categories, and you might have 1,000+ data topics. These are nothing more than directional numbers to help with the concept of the relationships.

As stated, the people looking at the data topics are going to care more about the rules than the categories, but this association makes it easier to maintain the management of the rules because the rules will be based on the type of data (data categories) rather than on a specific data topic.

This relationship also shows that you can complete the rules and categories (and probably have) before having any data topics. As with the other aspects of the methodology, this implementation allows for flexibility and for the implementation sequence to be variable. Also, like other data practices, records management can engage with the data topic methodology in a mutually beneficial loop.

With the creation of more and more data topics, very specific rules can be applied to a very specific and explicit set of data, just as it would a document. The process to retain and purge the data can be automated after this is set up. As mentioned, there is tooling that can manage the data retention and purge. While many are set up to manage a file, a database, or a table, the concept of a data topic is not out of the reach of some of these tools. The data topic is merely a label that ties to a script, query, URI, or some other method that was previously identified in the location and access method.

One detailed caution in that regard is the data topic that is managing a key that is found in another data topic in the same repository. This would equate to the corruption of another data topic or an "orphan record" in a database. This is not encountered frequently, but it needs to be accounted for. Some of the tooling available actually helps with that assessment to prevent orphaned records. When the process is automated, it creates a very configurable process if the rules or relationships were to change or if, for some reason, a data topic needed to be put on hold and not removed until further notice.

That shows the relationship between the methodology and records retention and how it not only reconciles the concept of a record but can make the process much more verifiable. So far this only accounts for the master data. What about the rest?

The rest of the data includes copies and the output of reports as we have previously identified. Depending on how you manage your data copies and the rules of your organization, you may have somewhere between 1 and 3 categories for copies. Each category would have one rule. That rule may already be used by other categories or may have been created for this purpose. One rule regarding copies is that the rule applied to a copy can never be a longer retention than the rule applied to the master of that topic. This is not to tell you how to set your records management rules, it is simply the nature of data topics and the SOR. If the copy was held longer than the SOR, the copy would become the SOR and therefore no longer be a copy. As discussed, a copy becoming a default master should be avoided.

Similar to copies, reports may also have an approximate 1 – 3 categories each with one different rule. A clear difference between copies and reports, and the master data topics is the impact of the rules on the categories. This concept is to make a type of data (that has become massive) easier to manage. In order to determine the number of categories required for copies, start with one. If you can say that all copies have one rule then there is only one category for data copies. The copies of data are only split into more categories by the number of rules needed. Keep it simple because the number of copies, systems, and people involved can be massive, so "simple" is very important. The same process is true for reports, but out of the gate there may be more than one. Financial reporting usually has a different rule than other general type reports, but that is up to your records management team. Reports might actually fall into master data topics depending on the type of reports. Financial reports might be one of those types if it meets the requirements previously outlined.

Now you have the ability to map out your data in a number of different ways just by combining the methodology with records management.

We talked about other slices of data so I would like to show a couple ideas of mapping out some simple combinations. You could map your data by system and records management rules, combined with type of data.

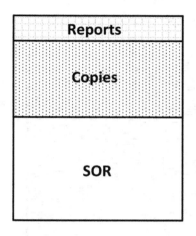

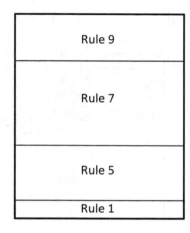

Figure 11-2   Figure 11-3

Each of these diagrams represents a single system. This may not be particularly useful to records management, but these diagrams can be useful to the ones managing the system. If you overlay these diagrams of the same system, you would see that all reports are in one rule (in this system) and the same rule is used for some copies of data. This conclusion, as well as many others, could also be built directly from the data once you have the data populated. Any given system could look very different from another. There will likely be many systems that have a much greater percentage of copies of data and many have much less or no reports. At a minimum, it is interesting to see the landscape of a system, understand how it is being used, and what resources and processes may be required.

The even more interesting and beneficial diagram is of your entire company. With all types of diagrams, the information will get more accurate over time. Just having data categories, data topics, and records management rules defined allows for the system teams to *approximate* size at the data topic level. When all elements are defined by *actual* size, the facts can be applied to the data topics. Since the system diagrams were of a single type, the type of system did not add much value to a diagram but it may be a useful aspect of the company-level data.

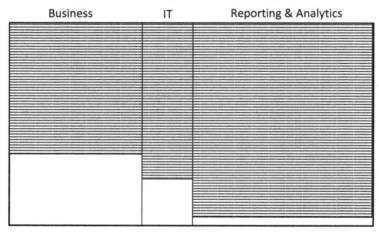

Figure 11-4

The shaded area in this diagram indicates copies of data and the non-shaded indicates the SOR data. There are many reasons that is relevant, but how does it apply to records management? By this diagram, you can see that the *vast majority* of this company's data is copies. It is very possible that yours is even higher. This is divided into the three types of systems that were defined which also indicates that the vast majority of SOR data is in business systems as it should be. What does yours look like?

The reason it is relevant to records management is that the majority of detailed work for data governance, data topics, *and* records management takes place against the SOR data. The copies need to be identified and managed, but they are bigger sets of data that lend themselves to different management approaches such as reduction of copies and alternate solutions. There are fewer sets of rules, there is less impact on downstream consumers, and the duration of retention is required to be shorter.

Across all copies of data, you maybe have 2-5 records management rules (this is not an absolute). The fewer rules, in general, the better and the easier it is to manage and understand.

You can now apply the SOR and defined counts of data topics and counts of rules to each data block to get a different view of the data landscape. These views can then be applied to other slices of data such as privacy compliance. When you are accounting for customer data, how much of that is in the SOR and how much is in copies? You only need to discover the SOR, but you may need to remove the copies. These diagrams do not solve the problem. The details of the data is what matters, but diagrams help for high-level understanding of scope, complexity, and impact.

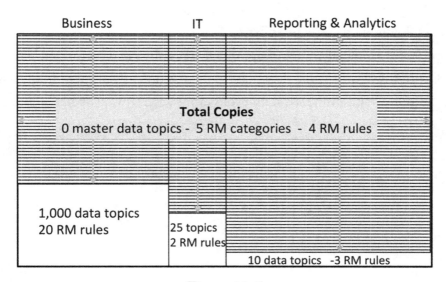

Figure 11-5

The numbers used in Figure 11-5 are purely examples and do not represent numbers derived from any information and should not be used as anything more than hypothetical directional examples.

If you applied the customer privacy discovery to this diagram, you should see a smaller subset of the lower left corner. The customer data in master data topics "should" all be in that corner. There is no logical reason that customer data would be mastered in an IT system and it should not be mastered in reporting and analytics, but it is possible to have drawn customer assumptions or profiles in an analytics system. However, if these conclusions are operationalized, they should have a master in a business system even if they are created in reporting and analytics.

Continuing down the path of customer privacy compliance, knowing that there are rules around the retention and destruction of data, the impact on scope and compliance can be significant. This is another example of two data practices being combined using the methodology adding value. When you have a common language and method of tracking, the benefits rapidly grow throughout the organization and the general data management effort.

Records management is not dead! It is alive and well and a major contributor to the overall data management landscape. It potentially has more power and influence than ever before when it is properly aligned.

Chapter 12

END USER DATA

We are not to the end yet, but we are getting close. Saving the best for last? I would not say that it is the best, but this chapter is about something that is bigger and more complex than you might have imagined. End user data and end user systems, in general, can be a nightmare for all data related practices. It is elusive. How do you possibly know who has what? How do you secure the data? So many questions, including the three questions and even those are difficult, at best.

If you were to throw the end user data volume into the company diagram of data as another system type, it would likely consume a *very* large portion of copies of data. It is even possible that you will find some SOR implementations in end user "systems". They should ideally not be there, but they cannot be ignored. If you find a SOR in a spreadsheet on someone's laptop, it needs to be documented as such. To this point we have talked only about "systems", but there are these end user "things" that house and create data. They need to be addressed.

It is possible to address, and without extreme measures; you will never have 100% control. One measure that many would see as extreme would be to not allow any local storage of copies of data. This could be accomplished by blocking the ability to copy from a system, other than copying to "approved" systems. Before going further down that path, I want to recognize a common argument. Some will say that, "at some point you just have to trust people". No you don't need to *just* trust. You don't need to disrespect people, but there is a business to run and allowing company and customer data flying around the network and onto hundreds or thousands of uncontrolled devices is maybe not the best strategy.

There are ways to technically put controls and monitoring in place, but before we discuss some of those possibilities, let's talk about the fallback. The fallback is also the first step in end user data. What is the company policy? There should be a policy regarding data on devices that encompasses all data practices, whether you can control them or not. Setting the expectation is required. After the expectation, the policy should include consequences and leadership needs to be committed to the consequences or you will be wasting your time. Is the company willing to terminate someone for having unauthorized data on their devices? I am not saying that this policy or this consequence is the only answer, but don't bother setting policy that will not be enforced. If data is lost or you fail a check for any compliance, what is your liability if you didn't bother to put a policy in place? It is not hard to determine that policy without enforcement is not a policy. It may even be that it is worse and is actually an attempt to deceive.

Maybe your policy addresses certain types of data, certain uses of data, the duration of storage of data, or many other things but it should be explicit. I would advise that you force yourself to consider the variations of scenarios and reasonable alternatives. I use laptop in the examples, but it could be any device.

Here are a few to consider:

- Is there any reason for anybody to have your customer's personal information on their laptop? If yes, who, for what, for how long?
- Has customer anonymization been considered?
- Who needs to have company financial information on their laptop? For what and for how long?
- Is there a need for any local storage (for most) or can it all be centralized data that can be better managed? How can you reduce the amount of local storage by people, volume, and type of data?

Somewhere between not allowing any copies of data on local devices and allowing any data to be copied is probably where you land. Not addressing it would send a pretty clear message that anybody can put any data that they access anywhere they want. As you make the decisions about what is needed and allowed, as well as how to manage it, remember the three questions. What can you do so that you can answer the three questions? How do you answer them for the copies of data on local devices? Yes, this is big because many companies will have no idea where to even start. There is a fair chance that the company has a policy (probably buried somewhere) about the ownership of data. It might even go further than that and state something about use of the data. Neither of those statements will get you the answers to the three questions. If you don't allow local storage, the answers to the three questions for local storage is easy, but you would also change the ability for a number of people to work until other provisions are made.

As stated already, a good place to start is with an explicit policy. The policy should be explicit enough that if it is followed you would be able to answer the three questions. There is a big "if" there, so what is next? You implement the technology that makes it possible to track.

The types of technologies come in many varieties including stopping copies, tracking copies, deleting copies after some period of time, and scanning devices for certain types of data. The first two are the only ones that would help answer the questions. The other two don't help answer questions, but are about limiting risk.

Use the example of customer privacy laws where you are asked to provide all of the information that you have about a person and delete it on request. How do you accomplish that with locally stored data of which you have had little visibility? You simply don't. How do you even state a case? Having a policy is a good start, but does your policy explicitly address it? Keep in mind that this is just an example and customer privacy data is not the only data that your policy needs to address. The laws are going to vary and the implementation is going to be unique for each government agency. Addressing this for your "systems" is a big enough issue, but the hundreds, thousands, or tens of thousands of devices... Are you running away yet?

There is no way that I can speak for your company or for the government agencies and tell you what an acceptable answer is going to be. Regardless of what you decide, a direction, intent, and execution plan is essential. The three questions still apply.

One of the easiest technical solutions is to extend the management of access to data to the ability to copy data. I say easiest but it will not be without challenge. Challenging people on their need for data copies vs. their desire for data copies will likely be part of the discussion. In addition to controlling the ability to copy, this brings up another challenge of access control that to some degree needs to be addressed by policy as well. Many companies will have reasonable access controls on their major systems (let's be generous and say they apply to all SOR data), but it falls apart in many cases with the copies of data. Someone that does not have access to data at the SOR may have full access to a copy of it in a downstream system. It is even more likely when it is a personal local device. Along with the other considerations for your policy, consider how serious employees think you are about the policy. Is the policy enforced? Are the consequences real? Would the company actually use them? Have they used them? What does your policy say about sharing information with others (those that do not have access to the data any other way)? If it's not addressed, why have access controls on any system or on any data?

Records management may have a specific category of data for local copies that could be considered part of the policy approach. What visibility is there to this compliance? Is it okay to just tell an auditor that you have a policy? What if they ask how you monitor it? What if they ask how you enforce it? Have you ever terminated a person or disciplined a person in any way for breaking the policy? At some point, someone will ask. I use the example of the laws and auditing, but I also want to remind you that a data strategy based on only compliance will continually spin trying to meet the ever-changing requirements. This approach also ignores the other benefits of managing data. The concept and purpose of data management does not change based on the type of hardware storing the data (such as local storage).

So far we know this about end user data:

- It is a monstrous scope to contend with
- It needs a policy
- It needs some level of accountability
- It should have some level of tracking or monitoring
- If there is going to be the ability to come close to being able to answer the three questions, some level of assumptions are likely to be needed unless all storage is removed from local devices

Technology will continue to improve on the possible solutions, but there has to be a desire, a will, and a plan with resources applied. It will not just happen.

Speaking of technologies making end user data management solutions possible, there are also technologies that take it in the opposite direction. There are plenty of reporting and analytic tools that create untracked copies of data by design on local devices. There are other tools that offer as good or better capabilities that centralize the data or even use the data from the source with no additional copies. Enablement of people to do reporting and analytics is essential to the company and I would not suggest that they be diminished. They should not be enabled at the cost of destroying the ability to answer the three questions when there are other alternatives in the market.

I know that I keep using the three questions but rather than listing the technical, security, and other detailed questions and requirements, it is a concept that most can keep in mind when looking at any type of solution or design. If it enables or at least doesn't prevent the answers to the questions, you can then address the respect and usability of the data. This is the same sequence that we discussed in Figure 5-1.

End users are usually the consumers/users of data. They will create reports and presentations using data from "somewhere". They are seldom the creators of SOR record data topics, but it does happen so don't ignore it if you find it. It would be nice to implement the same data lineage solution for end users, but with current technology this may not be practical. Keep the other options in mind and understand that a change is likely needed if you are to be able to answer the three questions about end user data. This is the most complex area of data management if you don't make some changes to process, rules, policy, and unknown replication and proliferation of data.

Looking at a logical approach to priorities, it has been stated that master data is most logically the highest priority. This discussion of end user data does not change that. However, your process of managing all data cannot be linear. Copies matter little if the original master data is not of the highest integrity. Working multiple fronts is possible with a unified set of goals in a data strategy. Understand your priorities but don't ignore things like end user data.

Chapter 13

LEGAL

Legal has somewhat of an ominous sound to it like security. It should. Near the beginning of the book we talked about data privacy and privacy laws. Compliance to laws is an aspect of legal, but it is not everything. The legal department in your company likely has something to do with ensuring compliance to regulations and laws. They will likely influence the direction of the compliance of the company and be on point for defending that compliance when or if it comes into question. With that role alone, it is logical that they have a say in the direction of the data strategy. They may not want to be accountable for it, but why would you ignore or not acknowledge the information that could make your position more defensible?

I do not want to come across as legal considerations being the justification for data management. It is, like many other benefits of managing data, one of the considerations of a comprehensive and logical data strategy.

In addition to compliance to regulations, there is also the aspect of litigation. Companies do get sued and data is critical to that situation. Data is subpoenaed and data is presented as a defense. The legal aspect of data involves governments, attorneys general, courts, judges, and generally adversarial people that are not on your side. How do you look out for yourself? How do you make sure that your data represents you well?

I can say that most companies would not want to have someone with my knowledge and opinions on the opposite side. In general, the court systems, the judges, and the attorneys are not very knowledgeable about data. Many are quite gullible. I am not saying that to insult or demean anyone; it is just an observation. Data management is not their forte, and to many people that do not have a good understanding of data and technologies it can seem overwhelming. The inherent overwhelming nature of data can be exacerbated by people that find benefit in making it seem even more overwhelming and confusing. There are basic rules, logic, and technology capabilities that can help remove layers of perceived complexity. When a person claims that it would be overly burdensome to provide certain data, that it will take a very long time, or that the integrity of their data is impeccable, many will tend to accept the statements at face value because they don't understand. They don't know how to challenge the claims. It may also be true that the person representing the data fully believes the statements, but when challenged they may not be able to answer. The concept of managing data that is in terabytes or petabytes and moves across networks at millions of bits per second certainly may seem like it is complex beyond comprehension to the layman.

As people start to tear apart the fallacy and bring data management into the light, things will change. Data management will not be just a term that can be presented as a facade and believed. It will require evidence and justification that can withstand *scrutiny*. The idea that "truly managing data is impossible" will dissolve.

I am not pretending that it will be soon, but I believe that it is coming about slowly and it will only take a few large cases to set the groundwork for others. Managing data is not just a luxury, it is an obligation and an expectation. It is unfortunate if this is the only driver for managing data because the benefits, aside from legal matters, are significant. And now we are back to the three questions.

How well can someone defend themselves or present data as fact if they cannot answer the three questions? It is not just a matter of answering the three questions but knowing enough to challenge the answers. A couple of examples would be challenging the meaning and the source.

Let's start with the location. Imagine that you are being asked these questions and what your under-oath answers would be. Some of the questions might assume some previous answers:

- Where did you get this data that was provided?
- Why did you get it from there?
- Were there other places that you could have gotten this data?
- How many other places?
- So you don't know how many other places this data is?
- What makes you believe that this is the best place to get the data?
- How many systems or steps does the data pass through before getting to this location?
- Do you have any integrity monitoring on each of those steps to get the data there to ensure that data was not lost or modified?
- Can data be lost during data movement, and how would you know if it was?
- Are there other systems that have the data closer to where it was created?

- Do all users of the data get their data from this system? Why not?

- Is the data different in other systems than this one and, if so, is the other data better? How do you know?

- Are you sure that the data is the same in those locations? If so, I would ask that you prove it by providing both sets of data so we can see if the data we were expecting is in another system.

- Do any executives use data from a different source? Wouldn't they want the best data?

- Can the data be modified in the system that the data is from? Is the original pre-changed data preserved?

- Is it technically impossible to change the data? Is there any monitoring that would indicate that it was changed?

- Have you ever had any gaps in data discovered in this system? Did it apply to this data?

The questions could go on related to the source and integrity of the data. Would a judge care? I don't know, but let me remind you of a few key principles. If the data source was chosen and documented as the SOR because it is either the system of creation or the one closest to it, and as the SOR, it is the source for all other data sets in other systems, then there can be no better source than the one used. Those two SOR concepts just answered a significant amount of the questions that were asked.

The remainder of the questions that relate to the integrity of the data are based on the "respect" aspect of data. Preserving the integrity of the data requires documented expectations and designs that prevent it from being modified. If it is modified, by definition of the element and the data topic, it is something new and would no longer be the same data definition. The one exception to this premise might be data that is transient, where the only existence of the value of the data element is at a particular point in time and that would have been when the data was extracted. This would be expected to align with the records management rules that were documented and could be produced showing that the history of changes is not kept and only the "current" state exists. As expressed previously, that would not be the case if, for example, a reporting and analytics system keeps all changes. They would then, by default (not design), be declared as the SOR for change history.

We have not even touched on the meaning of data yet in detail but the meaning, if documented at the SOR, has a consistent meaning as long as the integrity of the data is preserved. Let's try a few *meaning* related questions:

- Do you have the definition of this "column" documented?
- When was it documented?
- Did it have a different meaning before that time?
- Could it have been used for something different during the time period in question?
- Where, how, and when was this data "initially" captured?
- Does the date/time on this represent the time captured or the date/time received in the system that you got it from? If the time changed, what else might have changed?
- What monitoring or tracking do you have in place that ensures that the meaning has not changed?
- If your reason that you can be sure of the meaning is because others use it for that, is it possible that they are using it incorrectly as well?

Let's take this one step higher and add some integrity aspects:

- Do you have a data governance and data management program in place in your company?

- If not, it would seem that the company has not made any level of commitment to the quality and integrity of their data; do you know why that would be?

- Do you believe that data management and having quality data with assurances of quality is technically possible?

- Do you have any way to assure or give evidence to the court that your data is 99% accurate?

- If you could show that, do you believe that 99% accurate is quality data and something that the court should believe?

- How much data or how many records does your company have? Okay, smaller than that; how much data or how many records are in the systems that you used to provide evidence?

- Assume a quite small system these days consists of a couple terabytes of data. If the system storage size is 2 terabytes and the average size of a record is 2,000 bytes…wait, let's be overly generous and say that each record is 10,000 bytes which is ridiculously high. One percent off could mean that 2 million records are missing. 2 million. Is there any chance that any of those 2 million records are something that could impact this case or the data that you provided?

I truly believe that at some point the ability to claim that "it is too hard" or that the data is "good enough" will go away. It *is* possible to manage data. It *is* possible to know the answers to the three questions. It *is* possible to track and monitor data for changes or data loss and modification. It just needs to be done. The reason that you did not track and monitor will soon become an obvious statement that the company didn't care enough to spend the time and money on it. That would be a shame when the benefits to the company are many times over the potential risk and exposure.

In the examples of questions that might be asked, I did not ask the three questions. Not only do the answers to the three questions provide answers to the majority of the questions, they are basic company position questions in themselves. The three questions are important for a grounding perspective within the company and can help align the focus of a data management strategy. They are also like mom and apple pie that people will say, "of course, we need those answers." What happens when the complete truth about those answers comes to light? Answer those questions to someone that will not accept a smoke screen. Answer those questions about *all* of the data, *all* of the meanings, and *all* of the locations and what does the credibility of your data look like now? Imagine the difference of being able to answer the questions at the data topic level vs. not at all.

Companies probably treat their financial systems with a level of security and integrity because they can be audited by financial organizations and tax agencies and because the financial implications are obvious. They can treat credit card data with a high level of respect for similar reasons. However, the financial information outside of the official financial systems may not get the same level of respect. Why not? This is not to say that this is how most companies or your company operates, but you should know the answer. You should know the answers to all of the questions that were posed and more. Why would you not? Really, is the data not worth it? Are your decisions not dependent on data? Is your entire company not dependent on data? How much of your company's budget is dedicated to being able to answer three questions, treat data with respect, and enable appropriate and efficient use of the data? My guess is not enough and the percentage might actually be embarrassing.

When you are asked the question of whether it is technically possible to manage data and its integrity and have to answer that you have not done it, who is going to be able to answer the question, "why not"?

It's time to get off the interrogation, but consider these questions and more as real questions that you may need to answer with the truth. In addition to that, consider one of the first steps that set up being asked the previous set of questions; you were asked (subpoenaed) for information. How did you decide where to get the data and what you could provide? You clearly have to be able to answer the three questions about some data at this point. If you don't have the answers documented and maintained, you are making it up each time you are asked. What does that question and answer look like?

Up to this point, we have been talking mostly about the legal department in the context of litigation, but there are legalities that are not just about litigation or the legal department. We did mention compliance to regulations and laws but mostly in the context of privacy. There are many other data related regulations that may call for your data to be defended or to speak for itself. Audits may be executed against the location of your data, storage and access control such as PCI (credit card) compliance, HIPAA compliance, and many others. These require answers to the three questions as well as some aspects of respect. There are also financial audits such as data that relates to tax. Whether it's federal or state level, you can be audited and there are complications of tax audits that can go *far* beyond financial data. I could go deep into this but suffice it to say that most people have no comprehension of how much data an audit can impact. Depending on the size of your company, you will either have a tax department or hire a company to manage and defend your filings. Some people will think that as long as you have your sales transactions for sales tax and you have your income for income tax, you are done. The complex tax laws across the country that allow certain expenses, deductions, credits, and define the scope of impact in different ways, demand that you *prove* your compliance. One very important distinction in this category of defending data is the burden of proof. There may be detailed exceptions but for the most part when you are accused of criminal activity or sued for some reason, the accuser or the prosecutor needs to "prove" your guilt and you defend against the accusations. In the case of taxes, you have to prove your position or you lose. You lose means that you pay.

Again, depending on your company, the financial risk can be immense. Consider the possibility that you were not able to consistently and factually prove that your deductions and claims for credit were true and they were all rejected. On top of that, they may accuse you of having double the sales that you claim. Your gross revenue doubles and your deductions and credits are removed. Can you even comprehend the amount of tax that would be due and the associated penalties? Likely not, unless that is your job. If you are in an influential data management role, I would suggest setting up meetings with your legal and tax departments, as well as any other departments that manage compliance. Depending on the structure of your organization, that can include a number of departments when you consider all types of compliance.

I would suggest that at least the initial meeting be separate. I say to meet with them separately because you should gather their perspective rather than set up a debate. The various departments are likely to have different perspectives on one particular aspect of data management. This aspect involves records management and the duration of retention and deletion. These departments, as well as everyone else in the company, should agree on the need for accurate data that can be defended. You may want to ask about their trust in the current data management processes to meet their requirements because you may find that these areas have become another location for data. This emphasizes the importance of a centralized data management approach and a data strategy that accounts for *all* aspects of data usage and risks.

What if these departments decided to keep their own set of data for their particular defense? What are the chances that the data is identical or even sourced from the same location? If the data is different, what would happen to the defensibility of the data? I am not implying that anyone would intentionally do this, but lack of trust and controls can lead to unfortunate outcomes from good intentions. There is a reason that there is a negative connotation associated with the concept of "keeping a different set of books". Again, I am not implying intentional deception. When records, documents, and books were physical entities, there was a concept of the "master" and the one that was the original. The concept should be the same. Why would it be different just because of the storage method? The answer should be obvious; simply changing the method of storage for the information should have no impact on the need for security, integrity, *one* original being maintained, and the obligation and requirement to do so.

In this chapter I have tried to provide some examples of the "legal" ramifications of data management, but this is clearly not a legal tutorial and I am not an attorney. It is rare that an attorney is actually the one that has the information to defend the data.

While litigation and compliance are important factors, I have stated repeatedly that they should not be the only drivers of data management. There is no denying that these factors get attention so do not hesitate to use the motivation, but implement a comprehensive solution. Be prepared to identify and measure the other numerous benefits.

Chapter 14

PRINCIPLES

This chapter will highlight some of the key data management principles discussed in this book. You may see some of these as being rules, guidelines, or simple statements. Regardless of what you call them, you need a basis for your efforts going forward. You need grounding points from which you can set direction and make decisions. These also are good to use as reminders and discussion points to get people on the same page. There are not in-depth descriptions of these principles in this chapter; that is what the book is for. These principles are mostly labeled with the first time they were discussed, but related and more detailed information is scattered throughout the chapters of this book. While this list may seem lengthy, these principles provide a logical foundation and have relationships to each other.

Facts only exist in the past and require context.

The concept of fact is extremely relevant to data because often data is presented as fact when it is not. You may see this as being a philosophical statement that you disagree with, but read the first chapter and even my other books to understand the statement. The point is that, unless you can "prove" the data, it will be disputed and there is a chance that it is wrong.

- Chapter 1 -

Data has NO value without the minimum required metadata.

The minimum metadata consists of a label, a definition, capture context, and time; all are related to the value of the data element.

- Chapter 1 -

Treat data with respect.

Treating data as an asset is not enough.

- Chapter 1 -

A comprehensive data strategy is required.

The strategy must include all aspects of data and all aspects of the company.

- Chapter 2 -

The data strategy must be explicit in goals, execution, and measurability.

This is not a mission statement; it is a measurable execution plan. Measure your plan regularly and modify as needed.

- Chapter 2 -

All aspects of data management require authority in order to be effective and successful.

This position will meet with resistance. There can be no governance without authority and control, and there can be no data management without governance.

- General -

The data strategy and data management, as a whole, should be owned by someone whose only responsibility is data.

It is important that there are not ulterior motives or conflicts of interest related to the direction and decisions made regarding data. In order to help avoid conflicts with other responsibilities or with management, the data leadership role should be of a high enough level to circumvent those potential conflicts, e.g. reports to the CEO or the Board of Directors.

- Chapter 2 -

Use the three questions as your guide.

You need these answers to do pretty much anything with data:

1. What data do you have? (label)
2. What does the data mean? (definition/meaning)
3. Where is the data? (location)

- Chapter 2 -

Data management needs to be engrained in the culture of the company.

Understand that data management will be a culture shift. Understand the company's current culture and processes in order to align and engrain data management where possible.

- Chapter 2 -

Managing data must start at the point of capture.

Data security, integrity, and some metadata must begin at the point of capture/creation.

- Chapter 3 -

Capture only the data that you know that you need.

Resist the tendency to grab all data that you can get your hands on.

- Chapter 3 -

The best preparation for the ever-changing and diverse privacy laws and regulations is a good data management practice.

Don't "chase" laws and regulations. George Washington stated that "the best defense is a good offense." The offense in this case is data management. The specific direction cannot be foretold so be prepared by being able to answer the three questions.

- Chapter 4 -

Don't pretend!

Don't pretend to do data management. Don't just use the words. Data management cannot be just a facade; it will be a culture shift and there will be rules that people will not like. Pretending is a waste of time.

— General -

Communicate.

Communicate objectives, roles, expectations, rules, and the meaning of words. Everybody has a role in data management.

— General —

Breaking rules has consequences.

Failure to follow data management policy must have consequences. This is similar to not pretending. Managing data is a serious business and making rules and policies that are not enforced only damages the effort.

— General —

Be broad in your justification and benefits of data management.

A single driver, such as any type of compliance will just leave you chasing the next requirement. Document your benefits of known, managed, and quality data. This includes business relationships, infrastructure costs, labor costs, integration and management costs, accurate projections and planning, risk avoidance, legal compliance and more.

– General –

Know what the data means before you use it.

This seems so obvious that it should not need to be stated, but when you consider how much data might not have a documented definition or an acceptable level of quality control applied – it needs to be said.

– Chapter 5 –

Data governance requires authority and control.

Authority and control have been mentioned already, but since this concept is one of the most disputed aspects of data management, it is worth reiterating. If a data governance process does not have both, it is not data governance. Any statements of data governance or data management without the ability to measure and enforce are simply false. At this point, refer back to the principle of "Don't pretend".

– Chapter 5 –

Data Governance requires an organized process committed to overseeing the management of data to ensure its integrity and enable its effective and consistent usage.

Every word of this statement has specific meaning and summarizes the essence of an entire chapter.

– Chapter 5 –

Data management encompasses all aspects, roles, disciplines, and practices related to data.

Centralization of the concept of data management is essential to alignment of all of the data disciplines in order to move in a common direction and minimize conflicts.

– Chapter 5 –

All data requires one, and only one, authoritative source.

This is the concept of a System Of Record (SOR) and, yes, it applies to *all* data.

– Chapter 6 -

Data topics are the structured name for a group of data used in conversation and the management of data.

Data topics have a number of rules in order to make them effective, but they are the level of data that allows for specific information at a level above the element and below the entire set of company data.

– Chapter 6 –

Metadata is managed at the SOR for the data topic and inherited by its copies.

The effort to create/capture the metadata is focused on one location and all copies of that data inherit the associated metadata at all levels.

– Chapter 6 –

Protect data.

While protecting data is a subset of respecting data, it is worth calling out due to the diverse nature of protection that includes such things as protection from modification, deletion, theft, and corruption.

– Chapter 7 –

Only replicate data from the SOR.

You have the most visibility, quality, and control if you only move data from the SOR.

– Chapter 8 –

Do not replicate data unless it is required.

Only move the data that is required rather than taking more as long as you are there. Look for other options before replication such as accessing the data from the source real-time.

– Chapter 8 –

Replication is created and documented by data topic.

The data topic provides the mechanism to easily review the design prior to implementation and document the data lineage.

– Chapter 8 –

Create maintainable integration metadata (data lineage) with every integration solution.

Auto-maintained is the best solution, but even if it has some manual intervention with process, the lineage data is required.

– Chapter 8 –

Integration solutions should be reusable and as simplistic as possible.

Reusability is a priority because it helps ensure consistency, while simplicity reduces the number of points of failure.

– Chapter 8 –

Integration solutions have the responsibility for the integrity of the data from beginning to end.

The responsibility includes all forms of integrity.

– Chapter 8 -

Do not capture any metadata that you do not have a reliable process to maintain.

There are minimum requirements for metadata, but once you have a repository to store the data there may be a tendency to add more. Only do that if you have the resources and process to ensure that the data is maintained.

– General –

Reporting and analytic systems should not be the master for any data topic.

They should not be, but do not ignore the facts if they have become master by default.

– Chapter 9 –

A data topic is comprised of a data domain, a data topic component, and data sub-topic components.

The name is a hierarchical structure that is unique to a single topic. The topic contains a defined set of elements.

– Chapter 10-3 –

A data topic has a unique ID.

The ID allows for updates to the name without breaking relationships.

– Chapter 10-3 –

In order to define a System Of Record, a "system" must first have a definition unified across the company.

A definition is offered in this book, but regardless of the definition it needs to be documented and meet the needs of all aspects of the company.

– Chapter 10-5 –

Unify data management practices.

Sometimes various practices have different leadership structures that can be disconnected in message and purpose. The commonality not only reduces conflict and confusion but also enhances the effectiveness of each other. Look at the various practices such as records management, security, governance, physical management, etc. and their leadership structure. Unify them.

–General -

There is a responsibility for all data, including end user data.

End user data is called out because it is typically the least managed, least known, and least controlled, while being massive in its volume of copies of data.

- Chapter 12 –

Data is of no value unless provided to consumers. All consumers benefit from well-managed data.

Whether it be executives, standard reporting, analytics, operations, finance, legal, or any other end users, all benefit from data that is accurate, defined, and easy to find. Listen to the consumers of data, but giving them data with little or no management (controls) not only does a disservice to them but to the company as a whole.

– General -

The last principle above is certainly not the least important, but some may feel that to be the case when data management is put in place. While all of these principles are important, it is also important to keep in mind that the data is of no value unless it is used. Being used does not mean that everybody gets to do anything they want with any data. That is the balance of data management. Not every consumer will get what they want, but they should be able to get what they need. (I'm hearing a song right now). *It is possible to design solutions that meet both the needs of data management and the consumers of data.* They do not just happen.

There are a lot of principles in this chapter and this is not a list that you would post and distribute for the masses. This list includes some of those, but this is intended for those setting up and executing the overall data management practice. I am not going to tell you which ones are the best for you to distribute to the masses because the priorities might be different based on your current environment. I would, however, suggest that you create one that will fit on one page. A few good examples might be regarding "all data has a single authoritative source", "only source from the master", and "respect data". You can use these as a reminder of items that are in your policies which contain explicit language and are enforceable.

Chapter 15

BAD IDEAS

I will do my best to not make this the opposite of the previous principles chapter. It is inevitable that some may look like that, but I will try to focus on specific examples rather than generic principles. The bad ideas will proliferate over time as many of them are based on a few key ideas:

- Easy is better than right
- Why would I think about the future when I only need to think about today?
- Buzzwords are important and should be used and followed

I am stretching the statements a bit to make a point, but when you look at decisions that are made within your organization they may not seem like that much of a stretch. Let's look at a few real examples that have been presented to me.

Assign the ownership of data and its strategy to an existing leader (such as an IT leader).

There are a number of places in this book that make this statement in some form or another. I can hear the thought process now. "Why would a company need another leader? They already have enough leaders and one of them certainly can take on this data thing." IT is a common go-to organization because, after all, IT does manage data, right? The answer is very likely no. IT is touching and handling data. They store data and calculate the storage space required. They may be responsible for moving it around the organization and they may be in "control" of who accesses the data. They are often custodians of data, which has a set of responsibilities. If you have read the previous chapters in this book, I hope that you realize that is not *managing* data. Some of those responsibilities are components of data management but they are not in and of themselves data management, nor are they the foundation or a place to start data management.

It is very common to hear about conflicts between business and IT, but that cannot exist with data. The company is a business and, unless IT is the company's sole business, IT is simply one of the facilitators of operating the business that they are in.

Tightly coupling data to applications, people, or organizational structure.

Data needs to be its own entity. Data is not owned by any person, department, or application. The data cannot change when the relationships that might be associated with it change. People, applications, and organizational structures change and the data *cannot*. This is a hard concept for some to grasp. People that are managing data at a higher level, including those in data governance, need to be agnostic of all of those encumbrances.

"Good enough" is acceptable.

Good enough should never be acceptable. If you have better quality data than what you are using, why would you not use it? If you don't know if it is the best data you have, why not? If you don't know that the best data that you have is the best that it can be, why not? As you progress through the evolution of data management, you may have to use data that is "the best that you have" without knowing its quality. That does not mean that it is acceptable. It means that you should acknowledge that there could be improvements, use the data for what it is, and move toward the improvements. This is another area where pretending is dangerous. Acknowledge the reality of your data.

Daisy-chained data.

This generally has foundation in "convenience". "I know I can get the data from there." "I know who has it." "I have friends that have this data and I don't need to go through any process that gets in the way." "I can move the data cheaper" (of course with no integrity and tracking). I hope the downside of this is obvious by now and I would bet that it happens in your company frequently. Policy is the first place to set expectations. You also need to enable a method of access that meets the *needs* while not compromising the data.

"I might need the data someday for something."

This is not just convenience, it is the *anticipation* of *potential* convenience. If everybody thinks along the lines of getting as much as they can as long as they are there, everybody would eventually have all data everywhere. Some may say that it will never come to that, but I would suggest that it would get close enough to be a complete mess and that is a liability to the company due to all of the things that can go wrong with data.

Integration solutions embedded in applications.

Every application for themselves! So many applications come with "free" integration tools. They are not integration tools. They do not care about your data management strategies or even (in most cases) have the ability to align with them. They are pushing "easy". By design you should have far more applications than you have integration tools. Every integration tool now needs the capabilities to align with the data management strategy and provide and protect metadata. Does the "free" stuff do that? There will be push from some leadership to use "free". Be prepared with the explanation of why it is not free, but rather more costly. End users will also push for integration tools that come with "their" applications.

Democratization of data.

This clearly falls in the category of buzzwords. A company is not a democracy. Data represents the company. The data is the property of the company. It does not belong to any one person. The intent of ease of access is a fine goal with appropriate controls and design, but the implementations and discussions of this concept often fall far short of anything that resembles data management. This concept can actually be used as a position against data management by those that do not understand.

Pretend.

This is a direct opposite of the principles, but I could not resist. There seems to be many companies that like the words of *data management* and *data governance* but have little interest in committing the funds and resources to actually do it. They are using the terms as a means of communicating that they are doing something "good". If they believed it was good, they would actually do it. This ties into so many other principles. If you are not treating data with respect, making sure that data does not have conflicts of interest, and enforcing data policies that align with your strategy, you are not doing data management. Pretending that you are by using the terms will only delay any possible benefits and protection that data management provides.

"We have been doing fine without a formal data management practice."

"We don't have any data problems." What that might mean is that you are operating with blinders and have not yet been caught. It may be that you have been told that there are issues with data and don't believe it, or it may be that people are afraid to say anything about the data because they are sure that leadership does not want to hear it. Another scenario in this belief is that people may see operational issues that are costing the company significant dollars, but the problem is not associated with data. I would always start with the assumption that it is the data. The data is incomplete, corrupted, or ill-defined. People end up with bad information and make bad decisions when any of these things happen, but it is seldom identified as the issue.

This is clearly not all of the bad ideas that can exist. This is a sampling and you likely have your own examples. Keep the categories of bad ideas in mind:
- Easy is better than right
- Why would I think about the future when I only need to think about today?
- Buzzwords are important and should be used and followed

When you are presented with data that is inconsistent, it is far more likely that you have a problem with data than you have with an individual's incompetence. A problem with data can take many forms, but inconsistent data is most likely to be an issue with the source of the data. The next place to look would be lack of definition of data or a definition that is open to interpretation. The point of this being that if you are open to seeing issues with data, you will be presented with an opportunity to find not only an issue with that data, but you will likely find an issue with practices and behaviors that impact a lot more data.

Chapter 16

WRAP-UP

We walked through some basic concepts of data management. We talked about a number of terms. We continually came back to the three questions. The sequence was three questions, followed by respect, and finally usage.

There has been an emphasis on the need to have a means to talk about and manage data at a level higher than the elements but lower than the large buckets of "types" of data. There are some specific guidelines and rules contained in the methodology section that help to ensure the success of the effort.

I will assure you that if you understand and follow the basic fundamentals of data management and follow this methodology, you will learn things about your data that you didn't know. More than that, you may find things that surprise you if not shock you. You will find those things just in the process of answering the three questions. The three questions are a concept that all can comprehend. It is something that it is difficult to argue against. How can you honestly state that "we don't need to know what the data is, what it means, or where it is"? It is also surprising to many that the answers can be so elusive. It is very simple and yet so difficult. That is why a simplified methodology is essential.

To those that believe data management to be unnecessary because their company is successful without it, the measurement of your perceived success has no basis that is related to data. The measurement is likely financial, which is understandable and is ultimately the purpose of most companies. Was the perceived success *in spite of* their data rather than *because of* the data? What would the success look like if the assumptions about data were right and the use of data was actually consistent and accurate? How prepared are they for the future?

There is also the concept that being financially prudent equates to the narrative that, "if it's not broken, don't fix it." The problem with that is that most don't understand that it is broken. Let's use a kid's bicycle as an analogy. They have a bike and they can ride it. It gets them to their friend's house and they have never gotten hurt from riding the bike. It's not broken, right? The kid decides to sell the bike, which causes others to look at it. An outside view reveals that there is a paperclip holding the chain together. That didn't seem like a big deal, they would just replace the paperclip every other day. They couldn't tell what color it was unless the color was rust. The brakes didn't work well, but as long as you wore shoes with heavy soles you could drag your feet, and coming home presented a good final stopping point by bumping against the side of the house. The wobble in the rear wheel was only noticeable if you sat on the seat, but it was easy to remember not to sit on the seat because the seat cushion was a piece of foam duct-taped on and if it rained it was wet for days. The owner of the bike thought it was a good and successful bike because it achieved a specific goal. The bike was a success and financially sound as long as you didn't look at the time put into maintaining the chain, the cost of replacing the siding on the house, new shoes 4 times per year, and the occasional embarrassment of a wet seat. And what happens when a new challenge is presented for making a jump and the chain breaks, making a quick stop when a car pulls in front of you, or you are written up in the school newspaper for having the ugliest bike in the rack? What kind of bike do you have?

One other situation that feeds the lack of interest in real data management is the concept of time separation. The further in time that you get from the cause of an event, the harder it is to determine the cause. People may notice unfortunate or even bad events or decisions, but rarely do they get related back to the root cause of decisions that were made regarding data. Decisions might have been that one project that decided it was easier to use the "more convenient" data, or more general inappropriate behavior of data usage.

The logical approach will be a culture shift. The company may not be going into bankruptcy, but are you okay if you can't answer three questions (consistently) about your data? The answer, of course, is that you are *not* okay. There may be a few exceptions of people and companies that are on a path toward data management, but for most it will be a culture shift and culture shifts are not only difficult, they take time, consistency, and support. Don't be too quick to jump up and say that you are one of the exceptions. In my experience, almost everyone believes themselves to be the exception. Any attempt that is less than *real* data management is going to be futile from a data management perspective. Data is growing faster than patches, quick-fixes, or bandages can be applied. Running around making little pieces better will not only fail but will frustrate a lot of people because of the inconsistency. Some people will put major effort into it only to see it erode. Some will be annoyed by the effort because they don't understand. This does not mean that you should not try as individuals to improve what you can. Always try to do the best to respect data. The statement of futility means that if you are approaching data management without the minimum outlined requirements, data management will not only fail but should not be called data management. It will only do harm to future efforts that can use the failure as justification that it doesn't work. Are you and your company willing to commit?

Let's talk about the "close enough" crowd. Data that is accurate within 1% is close enough. You may find that your data is off by far more than 1%, but let's use 1% as a conservative number for now. Suppose your company is a 10 billion dollar company and you are off by 1%. That would be 100 million dollars. Is losing that okay? Is that close enough? But then assume that it's not off once per year but weekly or daily or even hourly or more. Your decisions are made on that data and the decisions compound on the variations and other decisions. Some of them, fortunately for you, may be off in the opposite direction so the impact might be offset to some degree, but that is not a plan. Is that a way to run a company?

Then there is the "been there, done that" crowd that has already been mentioned. They will say that data management does not work or is not possible because of previous encounters with those using the label of data management. There may have been similar stories of creating an Enterprise Data Model that did not work or was not worth it. I have heard a number of leaders in various companies state that "we have tried that, and it didn't work" when they talk about data management. The conclusion is that "it" was a waste of money. This is why the approach, the requirements, and the principles outlined in this book are important. In most cases (if not all) *it* was not data management that failed, *it* was the approach. It is unfortunate that there are so many failed attempts. It is important to assess why it failed. It is important to assess why it was even tried in the first place. Was it because of the vast array of benefits that were clear, or was it a single driver like a compliance requirement, or even as shallow as liking the way the words sound and the "impression" that it gives? Does that seem too harsh? I can assure you that many think it but are afraid to say it for one reason or another. Employees understand that they are working for an "at will" employer. Consultants that propose solutions have a stake in presenting something palatable. Vendors want to sell you products. People want to work and people want to sell. I am not selling anything (except for this book which you already have). I am sharing my experience and expertise in the hope that it will help, or at least give you something to think about.

Now that we are at the end of this book and various terms and examples have been shared, let me offer one more analogy that hopefully means more now than it might have before reading this book. We will move to something much bigger than a bike for this one; the earth.

The earth is all of your data and we could talk about high-level objectives for the earth in order for there to be a global benefit. That level of discussion, however, means little to the daily lives of the people inhabiting the earth. We can gather information about each person, but it is not reasonable to set any coordinated direction by person, apply unique rules for each person, or create categories for every individual in a group of 1. There is a need for something between the earth and a person in order to manage and discuss.

The earth's surface is made up of a large amount of water and 7 continents. Each continent is broken into a varying number of countries and each country may have states or counties, and states may have counties and cities until each area is uniquely defined. You can probably see where this is going, but let's go there.

We already said that the earth is all of your data. Let's consider the water (which makes up approximately 75% of the earth's surface) as the copies of data. We know that the water is a major portion of the earth and we also know that is not where the majority of the people live. Now that we recognize that, let's focus on land. The continents can be the equivalent of data domains. It is a grouping of people but most of the continent descriptors are about the continent itself, such as the size and location. This offers some insight into people, but very little. When we get to a country, which equates to the data topic component, we start to get more insight into the nature of the people and the direct impacts on their lives, such as the government of the country. We then drill down further into the counties, cities, or whatever level works for that particular structure. We can now apply much more detailed information about this level of structure that is relevant to the people in that area. This is the full data topic name and has a single location within a country, within a continent. The people will still have an address, which will equate to the specific location of an element in its System Of Record. Someone may have photos of that person scattered all over the place (copies), but there is only one real person (data element), and that is where the details of that person are described. If the copy has different information about that person, it is wrong. There are so many directions to take this analogy, such as other categories of people (slices) that can cross geographic regions, but I think you get the idea.

At the beginning of this analogy we mentioned the idea of things being of "benefit to the entire earth". While this concept is essential to the success of a data management strategy, it is not a reality in the world. There are wars and different approaches to government, economy, society, and life in general. Every government has their own approach to rules and process. This would be like every department in your company having their own approach, rules, and terms for data governance; it would not work. This is where the distinction is drawn between the people on earth and the data in your company. The data in your company is owned by one entity; the same is obviously not true for the people of the world. Single ownership has a clear advantage for your data.

Some may think this analogy to be a "stretch", so what was the point? In addition to helping some people visualize the concept of a data management methodology, it shows a pattern. Similar logical patterns often show up in various places for various uses. The logic behind this pattern is applicable to many situations, contexts, and subjects. You could draw a similar set of organizational layers in many places such as libraries, books, languages, schools, companies, military, etc. The need for layers to provide structured organization is not new. Applying rules to the layers and structure of that organization is not new. Applying accountability is not new. Requiring uniqueness and an authority of "truth" is not new. They are logical and essential practices and show up everywhere. Applying them to data is only the application of logic to a critical asset.

We have talked over and over about the basic and essential fundamentals of data management. You can make the list detailed, but if I were forced to raise the essentials to an even higher layer I would summarize with:

- Treat data with respect
- Unencumbered leadership dedication
- Authority and control
- Consistent commitment to the "rules"
- Use the best data

Many people will use quality and other terms in a way they feel fits their purpose and with limited scope. Quality, for example, should include all of the aspects that we have discussed such as well-defined, secured, and integrity-preserved, but to some it will only mean that there is a valid value held at the element level. The clearer you are within your organization, the better communication and participation you will have.

It has also repeatedly been stated that you are "pretending" if you don't meet the basics of data management. People can and do care about data without the company supporting *real* data management. They can make an impact, but the impact is very small compared to the impact that can happen from a *supported* data management program.

That should not prevent anybody from trying to the degree that they can. I have hopefully provided information that can help in that quest for *quality data* which is cost effective and available for use as "needed" for the benefit of the company.

All of this talk about the reasons that people will resist is not to discourage you from trying and moving forward. It is to share that you are not alone in your observations. Knowing what you will encounter allows you to prepare for the inevitable. Imagine what a kindergarten teacher would be like if they thought all there was to kindergarten was to share the lesson plan and teach counting and the alphabet. Imagine that they had no idea that kids would yell and scream, that they would talk back, and that they had far more interest in toys than in numbers and letters. Kids in the classroom without a teacher would likely be some form of chaos. A teacher with no understanding of the interests and behavior of kids would be unproductive. The teacher needs to be the adult that understands that the kids can have fun, play with toys, AND learn. We need more adults.

EPILOGUE

Whether you are your company's CEO (or any other leadership role), a data steward, participate in data governance, are responsible for any of the data management practices, or a user of data, I hope that you found some benefit in this book. I hope that you are encouraged rather than discouraged. I have personally heard the comments about my "controlling" behavior when it comes to data. I have also heard thank you from many people that have felt the benefits of managing data in a structured way. I have banged my head against the wall, as have many others in a data management profession.

This book is intended to help others find a path and to find a light in the darkness of resistance. Okay that is a little melodramatic, but there really are people that are passionate about data, about making data the best it can be, and about enabling the power that resides in data with integrity. I am one of those people.

I approach most things with a passion and dedication, and this book is one that I had promised others and myself for a number of years. It is a goal that I set and I am at the finish line of *this* goal. And now the work begins, getting people to read it. Data management is no different. There will always be new challenges and you will never be "done". It is a practice.

Best Wishes,

BIBLIOGRAPHY

[1] DAMA. Earley, S., & Henderson, D., Sebastian-Coleman, L (Eds.). The DAMA Guide to the Data Management Body of Knowledge (DAMA-DM BOK). Bradley Beach, NJ: Technics Publications, LLC. 2017.

CPSIA information can be obtained
at www.ICGtesting.com
Printed in the USA
BVHW051259091221
623633BV00008B/403